# An Elevated View
## Colorado Writers on Writing

# An Elevated View
## Colorado Writers on Writing

## Seven Oaks
### PUBLISHING

© 2011 by W.C. Jameson. All rights reserved.

No part of this book may be reproduced or transmitted in any form or by any means, electronic or mechanical, including photocopying, recording, or by any information storage and retrieval system, without permission in writing from the publisher.

ISBN: 978-0-9630829-6-1
Library of Congress Control Number: 2011903834

Cover and interior design by Sonya Unrein.

Published in the United States of America

Seven Oaks Publishing
Llano, Texas

# Contents

| | |
|---|---|
| Introduction<br>W.C. Jameson | 9 |
| Anatomy of a Story<br>Margaret Coel | 17 |
| Opening a Town<br>David Mason | 27 |
| Getting in Bed with Your Co-Writer<br>Kym O'Connell Todd and Mark Todd | 43 |
| From Pretty Pink Bows to Chicken Manure:<br>Embracing Poetry as Practice<br>Rosemerry Wahtola Trommer | 57 |
| The Writing Life: Fraught with Monsters,<br>Real and Imagined<br>Larry Meredith | 75 |
| Writing My Way from Effect to Cause:<br>From Journalist to Journal-ist<br>Mara Purl | 89 |
| Journey of Discovery<br>Dan Guenther | 97 |
| What the Hell Am I Doing?<br>Kathy Brandt | 109 |
| Cowboy Up!<br>Mario Acevedo | 115 |
| Writing My Way Home<br>Susan Tweit | 129 |
| The Writer as Shaman<br>Joe Stone | 141 |
| An Elevated View<br>Laurie Wagner Buyer | 155 |

# Introduction

## W.C. Jameson

ACCORDING TO A newspaper article I read not long ago, a large percentage of the population of Colorado is made up of first generation immigrants from other states. The great bulk of the newest Centennial State residents, according to the report, come from the upper and central Midwest, primarily Michigan, Wisconsin, Illinois, and Ohio. The city of Denver, on the other hand, has become the destination *du jour* for Californians fleeing the Golden State. In addition, economic opportunities are encouraging an increase in the immigration and settlement of many from the American Southwest and Mexico.

In conversations with new residents over the years, I've come away with the impression that most were intent on escaping from their former homelands. The Midwesterners tell me they fled the cold weather, the traffic, and the rabbit-warren environments of cities such as Chicago, Cincinnati, Cleveland, Milwaukee, and others. The Californians claim they wanted out from under the increasingly unbearable economic environment that exists in the Golden State. In Colorado, they all found something they liked.

A few native Coloradans and other long-time residents are sometimes heard to bemoan the influx of other people and cultures, suggesting the "outsiders" are diluting the traditional way of doing things. Others, however, praise the growth as an influx of long-overdue diversity. Among these first generation immigrants arrive many with talent, ideas, creativity, and expertise in a variety of fields, including the arts and writing. It has been suggested that such folk, coupled with the likewise accomplished natives of the state, all blended together with the inspiration of the spectacular Colorado environment, will enable the state to assume its rightful place among the country's most progressive.

Depending on one's perspective, diversity can be a good or bad thing. When it comes to the creative arts—writing, poetry, songwriting, music, painting, and more—diversity is welcome, even craved.

In immersing myself in the literary and artistic world of Colorado on my arrival, I was surprised to learn that a large percentage of the state's most notable authors, historical and contemporary, include not only natives but immigrants. Diversity. Regardless of where they are from—in-state or elsewhere—they seek to practice their art and craft, to make contributions related to their desires and needs to write. They have succeeded and continue to succeed.

I have long been interested in learning and understanding why writers do what they do. Why do they write? What motivates them? What obstacles do they encounter? How do they overcome them? What are their frustrations? What of their endurance? How do they persevere? What are their joys? How and why are Colorado authors different from authors elsewhere?

I decided to ask them. For this book, I invited each of the authors to write the essay they always wanted to craft on this topic, but were never provided the opportunity until now. I told them there were no rules, no limitations, and they were not to feel bound or restricted by anything. I wanted this to be an opportunity for them to express what they wish to share about their art and their life.

Why these particular authors? I selected writers who interested me, whose works appealed to my own writing instincts. I sought writers who were successful, and who had a presence in the state and in the nation. I sought diversity. I asked several members of the state literary community to provide me with lists of their own ideas about significant and important Colorado authors. The same names appeared time after time.

Native Coloradan Margaret Coel writes about inspiration, about where the stories come from. Sometimes, she says, they come out of nowhere and arrive with their own urgency. When they do, she insists, we must write them. The stories arrive in odd ways, but they find her. Coel begins her stories with the history, the facts. Upon these, she layers her tale, her characters, and soon a story comes to life, the history real and approachable. "Authors," says Coel, "move through the worlds inhabited by story people, live in their houses and apartments, walk down their streets, experience their hopes and dreams, see through their eyes."

No collection of essays by noted Colorado writers would be complete without one from David Mason. One of the country's best poets, Mason has experienced a wild ride to the top of the fiction world with his verse novel, *Ludlow*. With familial and geographic connections to this southern Colorado mining region and the famous massacre, Mason was compelled to tell the story of the striking miners gunned down by the U.S. National Guard. Based on historical facts, Mason interprets the violence and relationships of that time. He probes that particular darkness with a relentless curiosity and a deft touch. With his words he brings light, explaining "that fiction paved a way into the story, a way to ground it in the reality of flesh, not fact." This tale is anchored in the literary truth of Mason's imagination. He discusses the inspiration and process of writing *Ludlow*, then making his way through the tangle of reactions to the book from descendants of men representing both sides of the conflict.

Mark Todd and Kym O'Connell Todd discuss the advantages and joys of working with a co-writer. Mark is a renowned poet; his books and performances are inspired and brilliant. Kym has been a publisher, an editor, and a writer for newspapers, magazines, and internet news services. When the two team up to conduct a workshop at a writers' conference, the results are successful and always entertaining. Their co-writing career has resulted in two novels. They have also written two screenplays that are currently waiting for a home. For them, co-writing is an adventure, fun, and productive. They are always interested in discovering how their characters evolve from their two points of view. Rather than experience competition, they pursue each project with enthusiasm and revel in the fact that they are involved in it together.

Rosemerry Wahtola Trommer loves words. They "frame our experiences," she says. Trommer's life and her dreams revolve around words. As a poet, she says that words and creating rhythm are addictive. So much did words capture her that she abandoned her higher education plans to become a medical doctor to pursue studies in English and linguistics, eventually earning a master's degree. Trommer confesses to a certain obsession when it comes to words. Why poetry, she ponders, and not fiction or essays? The answer is control. She loves to "push poetry to its edges and see what it can do." Trommer views poetry not as a product, but a practice.

Larry Meredith came to Colorado from Kansas, and both states are prominent in his novels. Meredith writes of his evolution as a writer and of his own special journey into the world of fiction. Meredith recalls days when he spent so much time and energy dealing with doubt and frustration and fear as he attempted to negotiate the complex maze of the publishing world. He often asked himself "Why?" and he realized that he was simply unable to not write. The need was in him, part of him, and he believed he had something to say. Meredith writes of the importance of story, of tales peopled with interesting characters doing interesting things in interesting places. Meredith's love for literature and writing led him into a role as one of the organizers and producers of the famous conference, Writing the Rockies, held each summer at Western State College in Gunnison.

Mara Purl is a writer, a publisher, an actress, and a musician. Purl states there is something about being a writer that makes her stand back and play the role of an observer. Her first introduction to writing was as a journalist in Tokyo, Japan. Her editor became her mentor and she carried his lessons with her as she grew and progressed. Purl had an irresistible urge to chronicle, even as she became a successful television and stage performer. She writes of her transition and evolution from journalism to writing nonfiction and then fiction. "It's novelists," she says, "who crack the code on this ongoing progression of waking thought..." In fiction, she continues, "We can reveal [an] extraordinary, and causative, layer of unconsciousness."

Dan Guenther takes us along on his own personal journey of discovery from a soldier to a poet and writer. Guenther reflects on a quote from Fred Exley who said some writers write not just to tell a story, but rather write to discover the real story that lies underneath, the story waiting to be told. Guenther himself confesses an urge to write because of an aspiration to a more complete understanding of things. As a result, he evolved to a high level of commitment and determination during his pursuit of the dream of becoming a writer, of "achieving the superior in terms of artistic endeavors." Guenther credits his experience with the Iowa Writers Workshop as an instrumental influence, citing the opportunities to hang around famous and lesser-known scribes and listen to their tales of life and publishing.

Kathy Brandt wonders what a professional writer does when she doesn't know what to write, when the words just won't come, and muses about "… the times my characters take on lives of their own and decide events for me…." Brandt discusses the reasons she writes: For the experiences that ultimately paint her writing; to be published; because she has things to say. But mostly, she claims, she has no choice. There is "something in my chest, my stomach, my gut, that demands I write." She describes it as a "need," and writes of coping with the need when the words refuse to come.

Mario Acevedo was born in Texas, traveled much of the world, and selected Colorado as a place to live. Acevedo writes of how he reacted and responded to the numerous setbacks he encountered during his pursuit of becoming a published author, setbacks that included rejections and being ignored by the publishing industry. Despite the obstacles, he continued to commit himself and work hard. After seventeen years and six rejected manuscripts, he struck gold with his appealing and entertaining Chicano vampire detective fantasy-mystery series. In the first installment, the protagonist investigates an outbreak of nymphomania at a nuclear arsenal in Rocky Flats, Colorado.

Acevedo's story is one of perseverance. He took a writing course but proclaimed it a disaster. Undaunted, he learned his craft by reading and by hanging around with published writers.

Susan Tweit possesses a keen intimacy with landscape and writes compellingly about the importance of place. Tweit lives in and writes about Colorado. Residing in Salida, she is surrounded by mountains, forests, and sage. As she works in her studio, she can look out upon the landscape she cherishes. Indeed, the power and influence of landscape is apparent in her words. Feeling at home in a place, she says, "is not so much a matter of proceeding step by step in a liquid process, it is as much a matter of reading the metaphorical landscape of the heart as of learning the community of any literal land."

Finding and belonging to a place has provided Tweit's writing with more than facts and stories, "[the process] acquired depth and heart and a strength of purpose and tone that took my work to new levels and new audiences."

Joe Stone delves into shamanism, mythology, and philosophy in exploring the needs of writers and poets. Stone spent years working at unsatisfying eight-to-five jobs, all the while believing he wanted to write creatively. He felt a calling and allowed nothing to stop him. Today, he writes full time and is the publisher of an on-line magazine. Employing lessons from Joseph Campbell and others, Stone points out that we must have poets and inspired writers who will render us the experience of the transcendent through the world in which we are living.

Laurie Wagner Buyer, a poet and writer of great sensibility and stunning works, is known for her ability to capture her intimacy with the landscape as well as her daunting experiences and translate them into beautiful words. Living in solitude in remote and forbidding places she filled legal pads with observations, questions, and unrelenting affirmation to ward off loneliness and despair. She wrote, she says, because she "had to." To her, the challenge of writing was like that of scaling a mountain. She accomplished both, and achieved what she calls "an elevated view." "Finding the right words and working hard to perfect craft is nothing more than the ever-expanding process of going higher … of raising the bar for literary and creative excellence."

In the following pages, these Colorado authors invite readers into their creative worlds. The subsequent journey is equal parts adventure and inspiration. —W.C. Jameson

**Margaret Coel is** the author of eleven mystery novels set among the Arapaho Indians on Wyoming's Wind River Reservation. They have appeared on the best-seller lists of several newspapers including the *New York Times*. Her novel, *The Spirit Woman,* won both the Colorado Book Award and the Willa Cather Award for Best Novel of the West. Coel's short stories are included in anthologies and her articles have appeared in such publications as *American Heritage* and *The New York Times*. In addition, she has penned four nonfiction books on the history of Colorado.

Coel is a fourth-generation Coloradan and grew up in Denver. She currently lives in Boulder.

# Anatomy of a Story

## Margaret Coel

SHE WAS BEAUTIFUL, just as I imagined Sacajawea must have been. The sculptured bronze face and dress and moccasins shimmering in the August sun. She stood in the cemetery named for her—the Sacajawea cemetery—looking out over the rolling brown plains. The wind was blowing hard, I remember, the way it often blows on the Wind River Reservation. In a cradle strapped to her back was the figure of her child, Jean Baptiste, born a few weeks before the Lewis and Clark expedition left the Mandan village in North Dakota. She had gone with the expedition, the only woman among thirty-two men, an infant on her back. By the time she returned to her village, Jean Baptiste was eighteen months old, a dancing child, Clark called him. Something about the sculpture gripped me, tugged at my heart. A woman—a girl, really; she was sixteen years old—departing on a five thousand mile journey with a baby. These were the facts, and I knew the facts would never let me go until I had worked them into a story.

Stories arrive out of nowhere, out of a cemetery in the middle of an Indian reservation in the middle of Wyoming. It is always exciting for authors, the moment when a story arrives and we know we must write it. Stories come with their own urgency: they must be written *now*. We have to trust that it will all work out somehow, even if, in the grip of that initial idea, we're never quite certain how the story will unfold.

This was a phenomenon I had often experienced and never understood until I began writing about the Arapahos. They believe that the universe is filled with stories. From time to time, stories allow themselves to be told, and when they decide to be told, they choose the storytellers. When I first heard the explanation, I thought, of course. What else could explain authors working away sometimes for years writing stories that have nothing to do with them and that may not even be published? Look at the works of almost any author: Shakespeare writing about a Danish prince, or a Moorish general, or star-crossed lovers and doomed kings; Larry McMurtry writing about a nineteenth century cattle drive; Evan S. Connell recreating the life and death of General George Armstrong Custer. What explanation other than that a story had allowed itself to be told and had laid hold of an author's heart and said: You are the one.

What else could explain why, on that hot August day, I stood in front of a bronze sculpture of a girl who lived two hundred years ago and knew that it was incumbent upon me to write a story about her. It had to be done. I remember speaking to her out loud: What is your story? Tell me your story.

For me, a story starts in the actual world, a piece of information or random fact—a small kernel that might grow and bear fruit. I had happened upon a kernel, the fact of a girl and a baby and a journey, and something so poignant about it, so terribly human. But where was the entrance into the story itself? What exactly was the story and how did it want to be told? I needed more facts, so I began reading about Sacajawea and the Lewis and Clark expedition, getting a sense of the young girl with the baby, drawing closer with each book and article. I spent a week in Montana floating the Missouri River, stopping along the way where the expedition had stopped, camping under a field of stars that blazed in a clear black sky, listening to the river lap at the banks and knowing—*knowing*—Sacajawea had been to this place, she had seen these stars, she had listened to this river.

Then I found another fact, another kernel: a notebook had once existed. An old Shoshone woman had come onto the Wind River Reservation with her people in 1868. She had told wondrous stories, this old woman, about going with the soldiers on a long journey. And remember that the Lewis and Clark expedition was a military affair. She spoke French, and we also have to remember that Sacajawea's husband, who was on the expedition, was a Frenchman, Toussaint Charbonneau. She told about walking over mountains and floating down rivers in pirogues the soldiers had carved out of trees. She told about eating horsemeat in blizzards, hunting for wild vegetables in the warm weather, locating familiar mountain peaks and streams when the expedition reached the territory of her people, the Shoshones.

And when they reached the mouth of a great river and set up camp, she had gone to Captain Clark himself and demanded that she be allowed to go with the men to see the waters that wrapped around the world. To have come all that way and endured all the hardships, yet not see the great waters, she said, would be very hard. So she went to the Pacific Ocean. She saw the bones of a whale, which she called a fish as large as a house.

All of the old woman's stories are discounted by historians who offer evidence that the Shoshone wife of Charbonneau died at Fort Manuel in present-day South Dakota in 1812, six years following the expedition. They cite a notation written by Clark in 1828 that Sacajawea was deceased. The problem with these pieces of historical evidence is that Charbonneau was a much-marrying man. Even the historians admit that he had more than one Shoshone wife, and the wife who died in 1812 is unnamed. In any case, whatever the historians might believe makes no difference to the Shoshones and Arapahos on the Wind River Reservation. They have their own stories, they say, passed down by Sacajawea herself.

The wife of the government agent at the time recognized that the stories the old woman told were important. They were history, eyewitness accounts of marvelous events. The agent's wife started recording the stories in a notebook, eventually filling twenty-five pages, the notebook becoming more precious with each story, more laden with history. She had to keep it safe, she must have told herself, because she placed the notebook in the agency building. One night, the building burned down.

This was the salient fact; a notebook once existed that revealed the entrance into the story. I write mystery novels and short stories, all set in the West because I'm a westerner to the bone, a fourth generation

Coloradan. Stories about the West are part of my DNA. They forever capture my imagination, all those bigger-than-life Western people and the Western landscapes that go on forever and stun you with their beauty. I had been following Hemingway's advice to "write what you know" before I had ever heard of it. Now another story of the West had found me. I would write a mystery novel based on a beautiful bronze girl with a baby and a notebook filled with her experiences on the Lewis and Clark expedition.

I began by asking the what-if questions. What if the notebook hadn't been destroyed in the fire after all? What if someone had rushed into the burning agency building and carried it to safety? What if the notebook had been passed down from generation to generation, a family's precious treasure? What if someone outside the family discovered the notebook's existence and recognized its value? What if someone was willing to kill for it?

The answers eventually worked their way into the plot for *The Spirit Woman*, a mystery novel set in the present, yet intertwined with the story of a girl two hundred years ago, embarking on a journey with an infant on her back. But the story was also about the journey that my fictional characters embarked upon as they set out to locate a priceless notebook believed to have been destroyed, with a killer tracking their footsteps.

The stories that find me—novels, short stories, non-fiction pieces alike—begin with that tiny bit of information that springs in front of me, blocking my way and drawing me into a conspiracy to bring forth a story. One morning a professor loomed out of a black and white photo in a newspaper. All white hair and beard flowing about his shoulders and chest, a little stooped over with wrists handcuffed over his belly, being led to a waiting car by three or four men in dark, serious suits. The headline blared something like: Drug Lab Busted in Kansas Field.

A small article on an inside page, but it had taken hold of me. A professor of chemistry whose brilliance had gone unrecognized and had been unfairly compensated at numerous universities and scientific laboratories. But a drug cartel had recognized that brilliance and built a state-of-the-art lab for the professor in the middle of a Kansas cornfield.

Compensation was in line with talent: jets to Mexican beaches and Monte Carlo casinos. All he had to do was manufacture fentanyl, and he was very good at the task until the gloomy day the FBI knocked on the laboratory's door.

The idea of such a man—a small kernel—grew into a novel called *The Ghost Walker*. The character based on the professor turned out to be a minor character, yet the whole idea for the novel—a fentanyl lab on the Wind River Reservation run by an unappreciated genius—came about because, one morning, I happened to pour another cup of coffee and linger a little longer over the newspaper.

I've learned over the years that when this happens—a kernel springs in front of me—there is nothing to be done except to surrender because there will be no peace until the story is written. The girl in bronze with a baby on her back and the genius professor with the flowing white beard will walk through my dreams, dance about on my dashboard as I drive down the road, and meet me at every corner. And always there is urgency to write the story *now*. But now isn't always the best time. Now is when I'm in the grips of writing another story, and for me there's no breaking stride once a story is underway. So I make notes about this new kernel, jotting at a furious rate with the urgency of it all. I clip the newspaper articles, look up the books I will have to read, jot down the names of experts I must contact. All of which goes into a file folder that is now fat and overflowing, taking up half of a drawer by itself, a constant reminder of the stories demanding to be told.

I've also learned that kernels can appear anywhere—in a newspaper, magazine, book, on a billboard. I suppose I am always expecting them, always on the lookout. They might jump out from the present or from the past; they aren't particular about the century from which they emerge. But the kernels that come to me have one thing in common—they are connected to the West. The professor's lab stood in a Kansas cornfield, but the idea translated easily westward, where the remote spaces of Indian reservations had long been hospitable to clandestine drug labs.

But stories come to different authors in different ways. I've heard authors talk about the characters that walked into their heads. Sitting at an intersection, waiting for a green light, listening to the motor idling, and here comes a character. Not anyone the author knows or has ever met in the actual world, the character is someone new, a new man or woman born fully grown. The author Mark Spragg has said that, out of the blue, the image of an old man came to him. But the kernel that caught Spragg's attention, grabbed onto him and tugged at his heart was this: The old man seemed so sad. Why was he so sad? The answer that came out of that question led to the novel *An Unfinished Life*.

Any kernel or notion or idea, any image that appears out of nowhere, is only the beginning, the entrance into a story. And at this point the author's imagination must take over. To paraphrase Wordsworth, imagination is the art of seeing what is there. Not everything that matters is apparent at first, but that doesn't mean it isn't there. Imagination looks beyond the obvious and sees the connections and relationships that might go unnoticed. Imagination sees below the surface into the heart of things. Imagination is like a muscle. The more you use it, the stronger it becomes. When people say to me, I don't have any imagination, my response is always, maybe you're not using it.

For a story with a mystery at its heart, I turn my imagination loose on the "what if" questions, never censuring or blocking any ideas that come to me. At this point, everything is on the table; everything is possible. This is the time for ruminating, taking long walks and letting the story begin to play out in my head the way in which it wants to play out. This is the time to watch the story people going about their lives, like watching actors on a stage. Such surprising people step out of the wings and do such surprising things! Now why would she do that? Why did he go there? What is she doing here? You keep watching. You can't turn away because you are in the grip of the story. What is driving these interesting people? What will become of them? Gradually you begin to see beneath the surface into the hearts and minds of these story people. You build a relationship with them.

Stories depend upon relationships and connections, all the invisible strings that bind human beings to one another. Pull on one string at the beginning of a story, and somewhere in a following chapter, a character will cry. E.M. Forster put it best when he differentiated between facts and stories. The King died and the Queen died are facts, Forster said. But a story is this: The King died and the Queen died *of grief.* An essential connection exists, an invisible thread that binds the events and characters, and it is the author's imagination that sees beyond the obvious to that connection.

As an author who has carried on a love affair with history my entire career—I've written books on history; I've woven the past into every novel—I sometimes think that I might die of grief over the way so many academic history books are limited by facts. Lists and lists of dead, dry facts. No wonder kids think history is boring. Facts can be boring. The way in which the facts are connected is what brings history to life and allows Custer to ride again over the rolling hills to his death and the warriors to rise up and defeat the Seventh Cavalry, knowing even as they do so that in the very victory they will lose the war, and with the war, an entire way of life. How could any of this be boring, pulsing with life as it is? What is boring is the list of facts bereft of the author's imagination, bereft of connections, and consequently, bereft of meaning.

I am not suggesting that any author writing a non-fiction story about actual events jettison the facts. The facts must stand; they are what they are and what happened, happened. But I am suggesting that before writing any story based on actual events, authors must read widely and deeply and do the necessary research for the imagination to make the connections—to *see*—what the facts alone may obscure. Because Evan S. Connell allowed his imagination to see into the connections and relationships among the facts, a sense of the truth of what happened at the Battle of the Little Bighorn shines through the novel, *Son of the Morning Star.* This is the author's responsibility to the story itself—the responsibility to bear witness to what occurred in such a way that the reader understands what happened and why it matters.

By the time I sat down to the write the biography of an Arapaho leader, Chief Left Hand, I had spent four years on the research. I had surrounded myself with facts—boxes of filled notebooks and stacks of photocopies, hundreds of names and dates and events. But not until I began writing the story—which is when the imagination goes to work—did the connections and networks and relationships among all the seemingly disparate facts begin to show themselves. Take two events in particular: The Camp Weld Council, September 28, 1864, and the Sand Creek Massacre, November 29, 1864. The authorities in Colorado had met with Arapaho and Cheyenne leaders at Camp Weld and instructed them to take their people to an area in southeastern Colorado, near Sand Creek. The white authorities would then begin negotiations to make peace on the plains. But after the tribes had complied with the instructions, the Third Colorado Regiment had attacked the villages and massacred one hundred and sixty people, mostly women, children and old people.

What I had was a set of facts about two events with an obvious relationship. The Camp Weld Council precipitated the Sand Creek Massacre in that the tribes would not have been camped at Sand Creek if they had not been instructed to go there. But there were other facts, small and obscure—casual remarks in letters, reports of overheard conversations, veiled phrases in memoirs and journals—which depended upon imagination to make the connections that revealed the true depth of the relationship between these events, to see that all the time the white authorities were assuring the tribal leaders of their good will at Camp Weld, they were condemning them and their families to death at Sand Creek.

Strange and inexplicable, the way imagination connects the facts that allow the truth to shine through. But it happens because authors live inside the story, with all of their antennae finely tuned, as alert to nuances and stolen glances—maybe even more alert—as in their own lives. Authors move through the worlds inhabited by story people, live in their houses and apartments, walk down their streets, experience their hopes and dreams, see through their eyes. While I wrote Chief Left Hand, I lived in my imagination on the plains with the Arapahos. I experienced the hope and the dejection, the fear and the anger of a people watching their way of life begin to slip away. Story worlds are real and true, sometimes even more real and truer than the author's own because there is no place for story people to hide, no room for denials and circumlocutions. Even when story people attempt to hide from the truth, the author's imagination allows the reader to see through all the attempts at obfuscation to the truth of the matter. Nothing is hidden in the shadows.

In the months that author Jane Barker spent researching the life of Mari Sandoz for the novel *Mari*, she kept running into a brick wall. None of the facts explained a period of time when Sandoz seemed to have stepped off the earth. Where had she gone? What had she done? Why had she wanted to disappear? But in writing the novel, Barker's imagination saw the connections among the facts, and the connections exposed the truth. She knew how Mari Sandoz had spent the time when no one had any idea of where she was with as much certainty as she knew the details of her own life. And she wrote the story that she was certain was true.

Just as the novel was published, a packet of letters written by Mari Sandoz came to a Nebraska library. Moldering in someone's attic for decades, unknown and unread, the letters told about the period when Sandoz had needed to disappear. And they confirmed the truth that Jane Barker's imagination had discovered.

As fragile as air, stories, and yet necessary. Growing out of nothing but snippets of information or impressions that flitter through an author's mind—a beautiful bronze girl with a baby on her back, a crazed-looking professor with flowing white hair, an old man who seems sad—accumulating details that fix them in the world and depending upon imagination to make the connections, stories tell the truth. And it is in this feat of truth telling, at looking at the world as it is, at exploring hopes and dreams and laying bare the human heart, that stories speak to us and help us to understand the stories of our own lives.

**David Mason's** books of poems include *The Buried Houses* (winner of the Nicolas Roerich Poetry Prize), *The Country I Remember* (winner of the Alice Fay Di Castagnola Award), and *Arrivals*. His verse novel, *Ludlow*, was published in 2007 and was named best poetry book of the year by the Contemporary Poetry Review and the National Cowboy and Western Heritage Museum. Author of a collection of essays, *The Poetry of Life and the Life of Poetry*, Mason has also co-edited several textbooks and anthologies, including *Western Wind: An Introduction to Poetry; Rebel Angels: 25 Poets of the New Formalism; Twentieth Century American Poetry;* and *Twentieth Century American Poetics: Poets on the Art of Poetry*. His poetry, prose, and translations have appeared in such periodicals as *Harper's, The Nation, The New Republic, The New Yorker, The New York Times, The Times Literary Supplement, Poetry, Agenda, Modern Poetry in Translation, The New Criterion, The Yale Review, The Hudson Review, The American Scholar, The Irish Times,* and *The Southern Review*. A former Fulbright Fellow to Greece, Mason lives in the mountains outside Colorado Springs with his wife, Anne Lennox. He has recently been appointed Colorado Poet Laureate.

# Opening a Town

### David Mason

A GRAVEL CROSSROADS. Stand there at the X and place yourself, and maybe your *self* will vanish in the time folds of the land. You are someone else. You are no one. All being flickers like a lit match.

To the west a scrawl of foothills, mine shafts, canyons, pine and scree slopes. To the east a forested rise known as the Black Hills. Face south and a town grows in all the smoke of industry: Ludlow, Colorado. It is April 20, 1914, one of the worst days in American labor history. There by the water tank, just beyond the saloon, the school, the railroad platform, National Guard troopers have set up their machine gun. An officer looks toward you, then beyond you, through binoculars.

Now look north to the flat land filled with tents. A little city of immigrants, twelve hundred of them speaking a Babel of tongues. The tents are burning, most of the people fled to a broad arroyo beyond your sight.

This is where Louis Tikas stood, but who was Louis Tikas? A union organizer caught up in the strike and subsequent battles, an immigrant like nearly everyone else in the camp. He had tried his hand at coal mining and knew the horrible conditions in the mines. Four months earlier he had become an American citizen, learning the hard way how often this country is reborn in blood. He was a name acquired in far off cities, a young man of Crete who knew a bit of English. In the dark and firelight the shooting and smoke and soldiers were the last things he would have seen. That night he and Jim Fyler and John Bartolotti would be taunted, beaten and shot, their bodies left beside the rail bed for three days, until it was safe enough to haul them twelve miles south to the town of Trinidad for public funerals.

That was the Ludlow Massacre, or some version of it. You have come back to stand here at the X and lose yourself. You are a pebble of coal, a strand of fence line, a magpie watching from a post. The hollowing wind picks up a fistful of dirt and tosses it across the road to where the bodies lay.

Apparently the three men ran. They were shot in the back.

Apparently they were trying to stop the fight that had raged all day, but someone wanted them dead. Someone wanted to clear the camp. Erase the immigrants. On April 20 more than a score of people were killed.

Stand at the X and wonder who they were, and you might as well be wondering who you are, and what mark, if any, you will leave when the wind kicks up your dust.

Now I recall a Mason family reunion west of Trinidad at Stonewall Gap. Picnics on the Purgatory River. A clan of joke-tellers, leg-pullers, yarn-swappers. And someone says we should try to find Cedar Hill, the town where George Mason, my great-grandfather, ran one of the notorious company stores. The stores took illegal scrip instead of cash, upped the prices, cheated the miners—one reason they had gone out on strike. But the business got George started in the West, got him his toehold after he came out from Missouri in the 1890s, more or less.

So we piled into cars and caravanned into the desert under the foothills of the Front Range, looking for Cedar Hill. We found concrete slabs that might have been foundations. We found a mine shaft squinting shut, a hard-plated piece of ground littered with bits of earthenware, a fragment of a China doll in a faded dress.

Late summer sunlight glinted off the ground. Was this Cedar Hill? None of us knew. We stopped at the Ludlow monument where uncles told of the massacre, and I stood somewhere near the X not knowing it marked the spot where Louis Tikas died.

One of my great-uncles was born at Tabasco, back in a nearby canyon. His older brother, Abe, was my grandfather. By this time Abe lay in the Masonic Cemetery in Trinidad, not far from the grave of Tikas. But the story of Louis Tikas was still largely untold, waiting for Zeese Papanikolas to write his book, *Buried Unsung: Louis Tikas and the Ludlow Massacre.*

Like so many Americans we stood there gawking at a landscape without knowing its story. We did not know how bound we were to this dry, unforgiving land. It felt exotic to us, a film set without a script, a director or a crew to bring it to life.

We never did find Cedar Hill.


In 2007, my book *Ludlow* was published by Red Hen Press. It is a verse novel, which is a strange animal. Somehow the verse did not scare away readers. The book struck a nerve. I gave dozens of readings from it all over the United States, but the Colorado readings had a special *frisson*. When I read in Trinidad, a man admonished me for praising Zeese Papanikolas's version of events. "That book made me furious," he said. "It was so biased I threw it across the room."

Nerves are still sensitive concerning Ludlow. Some families are tied to the company, some to the strikers. The politics are raw, the scores unsettled.

I read in Denver with Scott Martelle and Eleanor Swanson, who had also published books about Ludlow. Afterwards a dignified gentleman with a gray beard came up to me and said, "I am going to buy your book. But I don't like what you said about my grandfather." He was a descendent of Billy Reno, mentioned only briefly as "the company's chief thug" in my opening chapter. I was learning about the uses of history in a work of fiction.

When I read in Montrose, Colorado, I met Dan Beshoar, whose father, Barron, had known my own father in Trinidad. Dan's grandfather and great-grandfather were doctors who sided with the strikers against the company. As a boy Dan had known John Lawson, the Scottish immigrant who organized the southern Colorado coal strike in 1913 and whose career as a union man was terminated by the Ludlow Massacre. Opinions differ about Lawson, but I admire him. After the massacre, he was hung out to dry by union higher-ups, reduced to working in the mines again with a pick and shovel, until his hard work was observed and he rose with stunning irony to a management position. Still, the miners remembered Ludlow. They remembered all Lawson had done for the cause. If Lawson makes the contract, they said, we will sign it.

Dan Beshoar has sent me some photographs. Among them I find Lawson with Mother Jones and Horace Hawkins, Lawson with Louis Tikas and one Robert Harlan, later mayor of Seattle. There is a photo of the "death pit" at Ludlow where thirteen women and children suffocated when flames overtook the tents. In another photo Frank Rubino lies on a slab, a victim of the shooting that day. Then there is the funeral of the children held in Trinidad at the Catholic church, not far from another church in which my own parents would be married following WWII. In photos of the Ludlow camp after the fires you can see scraps of metal stoves and bed frames, all that survived the flames. It is a bitter thing to look upon, no matter what your politics.

Finally there is a photo of John Lawson as an old man, standing in front of the Ludlow monument. A big man in a suit and spectacles, still fit as a boxer but with an aura of intellect about him.

"You knew John Lawson?" I asked Dan Beshoar. "What was his voice like?"

"Deep. Gravelly. Rough."

As a child Dan had sat on the old man's lap and listened to his stories. It was a baptism, of sorts, a ritual acknowledgment of suffering and rage.

Emotions about Ludlow run deep in families, in what children grown to adulthood can remember of their own flesh and blood.

Heading south on Interstate 25, you could miss Ludlow if you blinked. Not much is left of the old mining towns of that violent time. This is southeastern Colorado, where the mountains drop down to dry mesa country. You've gone south of the exit for Walsenburg, south of another for Aguilar, and you're maybe a dozen miles north of Trinidad, a far more significant town than many Americans, or even Coloradoans, realize. If you're on the freeway here you're usually headed to Albuquerque or points beyond. You're not thinking that pivotal moments in American history happened here: that Mother Jones was dodging the law to get into Trinidad and dramatize the plight of the miners; that John D. Rockefeller Jr., who owned a controlling interest in the Colorado Fuel and Iron Company, had hired Eastern executives to run his operations in the coal fields here and the executives hired detectives to enforce their rules; that Governor Ammons, a Democrat who came to office on the coattails of Woodrow Wilson, would panic at the shootouts between strikers and company goons and call in the National Guard; that the Guard would side with the company against the strikers; that President Wilson himself would be watching bulletins from the fight and after the massacre would put federal troops in place to stop the killing.

No, you're usually just on the freeway, which means you're not seeing much of anything. You're anxious to get someplace. You might be thinking the real Colorado is the I-70 corridor, which takes skiers west from Denver to places like Vail and Aspen. Many Coloradoans are new to the state and don't really know where they are. They don't know the names of the buttes and rivers. I wanted to find words for this landscape:

> A solitary cone of rock rose up
> from lacerated land, the dry arroyos,
> scars that scuppered water in flood season
> down to a river. In dusty summertime
> the cottonwoods eked out a living there
> in a ragged line below the high peaks.
> The ground was a plate of stony scutes that shone
> like diamonds at noon, an hour when diamondbacks
> coiled on sunbaked rocks. Or so I pictured
> in color films imagination shot.
> The butte they called *El Huerfano*, alone
> east of the highway. . . .We were driving south,
> and to the west the heat-waved mountains rose,
> abrasive peaks without a trace of snow,
> bare rocks above a belt of evergreens.
> This was my father's home. My father had

> a childhood here, so far away from mine,
> and knew of mines in the long-vanished towns,
> a butte the Mexicans had named "the Orphan,"
> and two peaks Indians called the *Huajatollas,*
> "Breasts of the Earth"....

Sailors know scuppers are the drains in bilges of a boat. Scutes are like the armored plates on an armadillo's back. I wanted the "sc" sound of both words for its harshness, an aural version of the scattered sunglint off the land itself.

It does not matter to me if readers fail to notice such effects in *Ludlow.* Some readers will read for the story, others for the words, still others for the interplay of the two. I'm a writer. I'll take any readers I can get.

Poets taking up historical subjects face many problems. One of these is the patina of documentary fact, which can flatten the imaginative texture of the writing. Too much political poetry attempts to accrue virtue by virtue of its subject, as if righteousness alone were sufficient for art.

I wanted to avoid that. I wanted the roughness, obscenity, and vitality of life pulsing in my lines. The immigrants who went on strike in 1913 were not angels. They were human beings. Scott Martelle has determined that in roughly nine months of skirmishes the strikers probably killed more people than the troops and company goons did—not that plenty of blood wasn't spilled on both sides.

I wanted vitality, not virtue.

Fiction proved a way into the story, a way to ground it in the reality of flesh, not fact. That was why I invented Luisa Mole and started years before the massacre. Her orphanhood—the immigrants nickname her *la Huerfana* after the butte I described earlier—is an existential problem more than a political one. It ties her to me, in a way, through a distant memory of childhood vulnerability. So I followed the lead of writers like Milan Kundera and introduced myself into the story, admitted my own motives as well as those of my characters.

Critics have noticed Luisa's name resembles that of Louis Tikas, also a character in my book, but have wondered why I paired the names when the two characters never really meet. Perhaps the two are paired through a third—myself, the narrator who occasionally appears, trying to piece the story together. The book arose from my sympathy for and identification with both figures. I used epigraphs in Spanish and Greek as deliberate clues that the book is about more than politics. I am standing at the gravel X, trying to know the reality of the self in this landscape, and I see this as the dilemma of many Americans. We move through the world as if our location were unimportant, feeling only marginally connected to what we see around us. Perhaps my identification with Louis and Luisa, one part fiction, the other wholly so, is an effort to understand my own complicated being. I am the X connecting these two troubled characters.

Of course my characters have more pressing problems than this—survival itself, for example—but they too live on multiple levels. They dream; they aspire. Their dreams and aspirations are lost in that fistful of dust blown across the road.

It would not do to have a photograph on the cover of the book, because photographs tend toward the documentary. The book is grounded in dream and imagination. The painting chosen for the cover of *Ludlow* actually depicts a California landscape. My friend Mark Jarman recognized this at once and could tell me approximately what view was represented there. That is fine with me. Call it an image of aspiration, an ideal unmet at the crossroads where Louis died.

One chapter of the book, "The Photo in the Photo," describes an image that actually exists in the Colorado Historical Society collection. Taken by Oliver Aultman, a Trinidad photographer, this image of a dark-haired girl is pinned to an easel and re-photographed, a perfect example of postmodern remove, rather like what I attempt in the book's narrative voice. But even that photo-within-a-photo would appear too documentary in style, anchoring my story in history rather than in the literary truth of imagination, so I set it aside in favor of the painting.

It is vitality I am after, not virtue. Presence, not truth in an objective sense. The problem of knowing will not be solved when the story has been told, yet I hope that a *felt* approximation will occur, something like a remembered dream.

If I write in any way for myself, as the cliché would have it, I write for the feeling of presence, awareness. I want to locate myself in the world, but just as certainly I vanish in that dust kicked up across the road. I do not know why the sense of my own reality has always been so tenuous, why other people have been more real to me than I am to myself, but this minor neurosis is certainly bound up in the how and why of writing. Here is a personal passage from late in the book:

> Windblown aridity in early spring,
> piñon, prickly pear, the struggling scrub.
> At noon my shadow pooled beneath my boots,
> my eyes surveying ground a step ahead
> for arrowheads or any signs of life,
> out walking a friend's ranch with Abraham,
> the land a maze of dry arroyos, slabs
> of pale rock, the flints exposed by weather.
> There too the terrible remains of winter,
> dead cattle caught in a raging blizzard
> lay unthawed in postures of resignation.
> I was so intent on treasure that I stumbled
> into a ditch and fell across the corpse
> of a calf the wild coyotes dined upon,
> a gutted leathery thing—it had a face
> and I started backwards, stifling a scream.
> What was I? Twelve years old? The age I dreamed
> Luisa Mole out foraging for water. . . .
> On our visits south
> I begged to be taken out to the mesa country
> as if those afternoons on skeletal land

put me in touch with some essential code,
the remnants of a people who moved through,
migrating hunters five millennia past.
Look for a bench, land flat enough to camp on,
a nearby source of water—there you'd find
the silicates in flakes, clear fracture marks
where fletchers made their tools, the midden washed
by wind and flash floods all across the scarp.
Nothing remained in place here. Even trees
had shallow roots. In dustbowl days my father
picked up points by the dozen on this land,
pot-hunting like his neighbors, half in love
with science, more with the electric touch
of hands across receded seas of time.
What had we found? I knew this evidence
of other lives had meaning of some sort.
I saw the strangers, grew among them for years
in my own mind. But was it love or envy?
Was it only pride of place? A kind of theft?
Always looking at the ground beneath my boots,
always listening for the call of Abraham
who'd find a point and let me think I found it,
whose meaty, sun-burnt hands would leave the pool
of wide-brimmed shade, point beyond scarred boots
to the perfect knife, worked like a stone leaf
and left there by the ancient wanderers,
original, aboriginal, and magic.

*Ludlow* is a book of evidence, not a concluded case. The only verdict is loss.

Still, a poet has to laugh sometimes at his own pretenses. I have begun a correspondence with Doug Minnis, a retired professor who grew up in Trinidad and knew my grandfather well. Doug pointed out he never heard my grandfather referred to as Abraham, only as Abe. I had to go for the biblical resonance, didn't I? Books mythologize as much as they tell the truth.

My father was the small town boy who got away. War provided him an exit from Trinidad—the Naval Academy, then Iwo Jima, where his ship was hit by enemy fire. He survived, married, went to medical school, moved to Bellingham, Washington, where I was born and raised. But Trinidad was never far from us in family lore with its dry mesas and Purgatory River. I loved going there. I loved seeing Abe and Ethel, my loquacious grandmother, my Uncle Frank and his four children.

Frank could tell a story like nobody else. He told me about the old dance hall in town with a floor on giant springs to absorb the traffic of shuffling feet—the very floor where Louis Tikas may have danced with Pearl Jolly, a married woman with whom he is rumored to have had an affair. As a boy, Frank rode rodeo until a bull threw him in the dirt. "Peeled off the whole front of my face," Frank said with a cigarette laugh. "Boy, I walked around for weeks and the whole front of my face was one big scab." It's cowboy hyperbole. To Frank we were equals in the kingdom of laughter. "That old boy," he said of someone else, "he looked like he'd been drug through a knothole."

Frank liked to fix things. In the war he fixed airplane engines on a Pacific island. He came home in his sailor suit, married Margie, and went to work for Abe at the candy company. On hot summer days he rolled a pack of cigarettes up, sailor-fashion, in the short sleeve of his T-shirt.

The Mason Candy Company had a brand name, Tomah, and a logo depicting an adobe pueblo. It made hard candy and chocolate mints and a few specialty items, selling them in southeastern Colorado and the bordering states. Frank worked as a drummer at first, and years later he told how he opened up a town. He drove into some dusty place in Kansas or Oklahoma, cruised up and down the streets to check out the competition. Then he booked himself a motel room, sat on the edge of the bed with the phone book on his lap and started cold-calling stores that might sell candy, making good use of his gift for the gab.

Writing a book like *Ludlow* is a bit like opening up a town, trying to make contact with a place, find out who lives there, charm them into buying what you've got to sell. I have always thought writing should be tied to the way people talk. The further writing moves from actual speech, the more removed it is from vitality. Often the voice I heard in my head was Frank's, often my father's, sometimes Abe's.

Late on a Saturday night in Trinidad, Frank and Marge came home from some motel where she had played bass and he drums in a jazz combo, and they had danced when others sat in, and smoked their voices raw. I remember loving it when they came home and laughter filled the house on Victoria Square and nobody cared the kids were still awake. My own parents were moving toward divorce and a shell of alienation covered each of us, but in Frank's house there always seemed to be the coherence of family.

I'm standing at the X again. X marks the spot. Dust devils cross the road.

When Abe died Frank took over the company, but he ran into bad luck. After Marge's sudden death and the failure of the business, Frank moved north of Denver. He remarried and lived in the trailer in Longmont. Not long after Alzheimer's killed my father, cancer and heart trouble got Frank. The other two brothers, Jack and Tom, are gone now as well. The four redheaded Mason boys of Trinidad, Colorado are dead.

The only verdict is loss.


Writing *Ludlow* in verse, I knew I had some precedents from Homer to the present day. Contemporary poets like Brad Leithauser, Glyn Maxwell and Les Murray had all written novels in verse. But *Ludlow* is not easy to define. It is not quite a novel, not quite an epic in the classical sense. Reviewers and readers have been kind to it, but my fellow poets do not always know what to make of it. Sometimes a book does not behave as we expect it to, and maybe it is all right that *Ludlow* perplexes the literati. It is a book I had to write when I had to write it. It is everything I knew at the time about Colorado, about stories and about poetry. So be it. After years of reading and thought I felt an accumulation of energy and knew it was a book. I read about Louis Tikas, born Ilias Spantidakis in Crete, and I knew something of his story because I have lived in Greece, speak reasonable Greek, and have many friends caught up in the double-consciousness of the immigrant, the way you dream in one language and wake to another.

When I invented a Scotsman named Too Tall MacIntosh who would join the strikers, I was in part remembering my own Scottish ancestry. But I was also recalling John Lennox, my beloved father-in-law, who had brought his wife and two daughters to America. When I wrote the book, John's widow, Hetty, was living under our roof, shyly regaling us with Ayrshire memories.

"Hetty, there's a full moon tonight. Tell us what you did back home on the night of a full moon."

"Oh, the full moon—that was when we went to visit the neighbors."

They needed a full moon to see their way home in the dark.

I laced the language of *Ludlow* with Scots, bits of Greek and Spanish, because I wanted a texture of words as wealthy as the stories of the place. I wanted, as far as my powers could manage it, an enrichment of American idioms, not from books but from talk.

The way John Lennox used to talk about Bobbie Burns—"That man had th' advantage o' the Scottish dialect as well as the English language"—guided me as much as my own reading of other dialect writers. Among those writers I would list Derek Walcott, so gifted with the macaronic language of his Caribbean island home. Whether my resolution succeeded or failed is out of my hands now.


Abe and Ethel Mason lie a little ways to the north of Louis Tikas in the Masonic Cemetery of Trinidad. When I stand at Louis's grave, Fisher's Peak is off to the east, one of the most beautiful flat-topped mesas in the American West, with the sleepy town at its foot. Surrounding Louis's grave are headstones inscribed in Japanese, Hungarian, Polish, Italian.... This story is part of America's story. The local is national. The ordinary is extraordinary. American poets are constantly rediscovering such things.

Whatever my literary influences, whatever I have imitated over the years, I can only write poems out of my own DNA, much as I want to achieve something akin to the work of poets I admire. I choose my material and methods, but something of what I write was set before I was born. It is my blood, my inheritance—recognized more than chosen—something to do with that fellow standing where X marks the spot, the fellow who would open up a vanished town and populate it with the living and the dead.

No person is ever really one thing. I am paraphrasing John Donne here, each man a part of the main. Is there a subterranean relatedness between us that we too often forget? I am Louis and Luisa, though historians will remind me that Louis was his own man, thank you very much. Zeese Papanikolas tells me the Cretan was probably tougher and more militant than I have made him. Perhaps I have taken some part of him on, some part of the real Louis Tikas, and made use of him as willfully as I have used the landscape:

> This singular man. This footnote nearly lost
> from pages of the history books. Louis-
> Ilias, named for the fiery prophet,
> but often so uncertain of his skin
> that only someone else's touch, some whore
> who thought he was Sicilian or a Serb,
> and took the money first and said no kissing,
> made him believe that he was truly alive. . . .
> What does it mean, nation of immigrants?
> What are the accents, fables, voices of roads,
> the tall tales told by the smallest desert plants?
> Even the wind in barbed wire goads
> me into making lines, fencing my vagrant thought.
> A story is the language of desire.
> A journey home is never what it ought
> to be.
>     A land of broken glass. Of gunfire.

My own need for intimacy is implicated in what I write—a desire to be known or understood or simply touched. Writing is a regression to vulnerable states as well as an assertion of powers beyond ourselves. Yet in *Ludlow* I am not merely being confessional. Events did take place. Forces were arrayed in the bloody American story. People lived and died. David Mason, whoever the hell he is, forms a very, very small part of the tale.

Q: What is a Colorado poet?
A: A poet who lives in Colorado.
Q: What is a Western poet?
A: A poet who lives in the West, especially one born and raised there.
Q: What is the West?
A: Rivers and mountains and myths.
But I have lived in many places.

I identify at some times with the vanishing self at the crossroads, at others with glaciers and mossy firs, at others with the Aegean Sea. Like anyone else, I suppose, I know what it means to shape-shift. I am less than what I love, less than what I admire. Telling a story, I am related to all storytellers everywhere. Telling it in verse adds a bit of charge, another layer of awareness, and connects my small effort to ancient impulses. A poet is more than a throbbing wound. A poet is also a drummer on the road, trying to open up a town.

**Kym O'Connell Todd and Mark Todd** are co-authors of *The Silverville Swindle* (Ghost Road Press) and the forthcoming *The Silverville Pantiwyckes*. Kym has served as a publisher, editor, and writer for newspapers, magazines, and internet news services. Mark teaches creative writing at Western State College in Gunnison and has two books of poetry, *Wire Song* (Conundrum Press) and *Tamped, But Loose Enough to Breathe* (Ghost Road Press). They live in a Western Colorado ranching community with five horses, three dogs, and six worthless house cats. They spend most of their time feeding animals and all of their money on veterinary bills. Ever looking for the offbeat, the Todds also study ancient Egyptian hieroglyphics and Middle Eastern drumming. They argue constantly about what happened at Roswell. With Larry Meredith, they organize and conduct the popular Writing the Rockies writers' conference in Gunnison.

# Getting in Bed with Your Co-Writer

### Kym O'Connell Todd and Mark Todd

FOR US, SUCCESSFUL collaborative writing is like good sex.

First comes foreplay: we begin to brainstorm, teasing out seductive story lines to see if there's something we both want to spend time developing. And we've been doing this long enough that we already have a pretty good idea of what turns on our partner. As the passion for our story builds, we become excited as character and plot flesh out. We then get into the rhythm of storytelling, thrusting ideas from our sweaty little brains deep into the body of our tale. The heat finally culminates in an orgasmic release when we write the words "The End."

But before you rush out to find a co-writer, remember that not everyone is going to be a willing (or a satisfactory) partner. The chemistry has to work. That doesn't necessarily mean you have to find someone who's good in bed, but rather someone who possesses similar mental, emotional, and professional writing compatibilities. One of the greatest advantages to co-writing is that two minds are always better than one when it comes to solving problems and bouncing ideas off one another. One person can temper the other. A plot point may not sound as workable when it's verbalized to a co-author.

Of course, everyone engages in some level of co-writing to get that story into print. Even adamant solitary writers. Agents, editors, and publishers are all going to give their two cents' worth, and you're going to want to listen to at least some of it. Once your work reaches the hands of readers, and you develop an audience, you'll want to consider what works for them so they continue to support your habit. That doesn't mean that you sacrifice the integrity of your writing, but you'll want to tailor your books to sell. A good friend of ours had a collection of short stories accepted by a university press, but after they insisted on drastic changes, he withdrew the collection. In this case, the two failed to strike a satisfactory partnership. When he finally found the right press for his words, did they suggest changes? Sure, but they were ones he thought improved the overall work.

In yet another situation, a publisher paired a different friend of ours, a well-published science fiction author, with an aeronautics specialist. The specialist focused meticulously on the science while our friend just wanted to tell a good tale. Inflated egos weighed heavily on the whole project, and we listened to our friend complain for a year as the book trudged toward publication.

As in all forms of co-writing, ego has to go out the window. No drama queens or kings allowed. If you're going to partner up with another author for that next book, you both must feel free to offer ideas the other can shoot down or spin in a different direction. Ideally, neither party takes offense. Both authors must possess similar work ethics, demonstrate a willingness to meet deadlines, and stay on task. Think of Douglas Preston and Lincoln Child, the writing duo who created *The Relic*, *The Cabinet of Curiosities*, and multiple other page-turning thrillers. And they live half a continent apart.

How do they do it? You'll have to ask them. But we suspect they use an electronic version of "transom writing." Transoms are those windows over doors that open for ventilation. You've seen them; they're in virtually every old schoolhouse across the nation. In transom writing, each author writes a passage and then passes it on to the co-writer, who then takes responsibility for writing the next section. They exchange drafts back and forth like circulating air through a transom. It's a kind of turn writing. Preston and Child co-author some books and individually author others. And they do it all well. Still, in their collaborative projects, we can spot now and then a subtle change of voices among chapters—a shift in favorite vocabulary and rhythms of syntax. That's what tells us they're turn writing.

We don't do that.

We're a lot more intimate in our approach.

Our readers tell us they can't detect any shift in voice in our writing. That's because there isn't any.

> Fade In.
> *Kym and Mark sit on the bed, crouched over a laptop. Mark types as they talk.*
> Kym. [Dictating.] Pleasance stood atop the Pyramid of Kukulcán, hoping to –
> Mark. [Interrupting.]—escape the sticky mid-summer—
> Kym. [Interrupting.]—swelter.
> Mark. Yeah, I like that. And then how about, Trying to ignore the sweat that pooled at her bosom.
> Kym. No, change that to between her breasts.
> *Mark deletes and retypes.*
> Kym. And we need to describe the jungle before we get to the sweaty breasts.
> *Mark moves the cursor to the end of the first sentence.*
> Mark [Typing.] The Yucatán jungle stretched in all directions, islands of—
> Kym.—stone ruins occasionally interrupting the monotonous green—
> Mark.—of dwarfed cedar and chakah trees.
> *They give each other a high five.*
> Fade Out.

Okay, that may not have been exactly the way we wrote that particular passage from our novel, *The Silverville Pantiwyckes*, but it's how we co-author—one of us starts a sentence and the other finishes it. Plus, Mark is dyslexic and Kym catches misspellings as we go along. (We're doing it right now as we type this article.) In our case, Mark is the typist because Kym can't use the touch pad on the laptop. It's all pretty efficient except when one of our six house cats jumps on the keyboard. There's nothing transom-like in the way we compose at the sentence level. And this technique allows us to test out loud as we go along just how naturally the words flow on the page.

We'd be the first to admit this is probably not the fastest way to write for most people. But it works for us because we like to write together, and we decide up front on a project that we both feel passionate about. The biggest challenge, of course, is to find or block out regular periods of time when we're both available. Kym is an early-morning person (she's up before the sun) while Mark isn't even coherent until 11 a.m. Our best compromise falls midday, and we plan accordingly.

It also helps that we both have equally twisted senses of humor. In our first novel, *The Silverville Swindle*, we have a scene where the sheriffs of two counties meet to decide jurisdiction over unidentified human remains found more or less straddling the line:

> "It's not Silver County's problem," Carl said at last.
> "Wait a minute!" the other sheriff objected. "You guys found as many bones on your side as we did."
> "C'mon, Andy, you've got the skull," Carl said. "That officially gives you more bone mass than we have."
> "Yeah, but you guys have the teeth."
> "We don't know for sure those dentures are that fellow's teeth. Maybe somebody was out here hiking and dropped them." Carl looked pretty satisfied with his deduction.
> "Oh man, that ain't right. We had to bury one earlier this spring. You haven't had one in a couple of years."
> They argued back and forth for several minutes . . .

This scene was a howl to write, and we were having too much fun to worry much about whether or not readers would agree. We enjoy this type of book, and we hoped the same kind of readers would discover our novel. More important to us was writing true to what we thought was funny.

The best writers say to write what you know. That's exactly what we did with *Silverville*. We drew upon real personalities and real situations that we've experienced or heard about living in the mountainous West. The scene above—or something close—actually took place between Gunnison and an adjoining county. To be truthful, nearly all of the situations in our book happened somewhere in at least one of our pasts.

For instance, we inserted an anecdote where townsfolk flee from an apparently rabid dog with a frothing mouth. That dog, in reality, was Kym's childhood pet. "Roscoe" had helped himself to a meringue pie cooling on someone's front steps. The dog scared the wits out of the neighborhood until the cook discovered her empty pie plate.

Another scene in the book has a real sense of authenticity since Mark's family owned a mortuary business:

> *Buford gawked at the open shelves neatly stacked with rows of embalming fluid bottles, instruments, and linens. He'd never been in the room long enough before to get a close look at the mysterious equipment kept there. Picking up a cardboard box, he plucked out a small pink disc that was shaped like half a hollow marble.*
> 
> *"What are these?"*
> 
> *Howard dropped his towel into a hamper. "They're eye cups. We stick them under the eyelids after someone dies." Then he added, "So the eyes won't sink."*
> 
> *Buford took two of the little cups and raised them to his own eyes, squinting to hold them in place like two plastic monocles. "Like this?"*
> 
> *He heard the door open behind him and turned, blindly, in that direction.*
> 
> *"Buford, what are you doing in here?"*
> 
> *Opening his eyes, Buford felt the cups slide down his cheeks toward the floor. Denton stood with his hands on his hips, and he didn't look pleased.*

Of course, Mark never played with eye cups. (At least, he never got caught.)

The advantage should be obvious—two heads mean two sets of experiences. It also means two sets of critical eyes because we each bring to the Writing Bed individual strengths that mitigate the individual weaknesses. Kym's journalism background makes her succinct to a fault. Mark, on the other hand, comes from the halls of academia and doesn't know when to quit. Somewhere between these two extremes is the point we shoot for using each other's complementary strengths.

Kym has a keen ear for dialog: she can hear the way different characters should talk, and the result is a distinct voice for each. Mark's characters all tend to talk just like Mark. But Mark bravely jumps right into a scene, while Kym endlessly stares at the screen waiting for the right words to come. Kym constantly plays devil's advocate when it comes to defending the reader's willing suspension of disbelief. If she can't buy it, she won't let it happen. Mark, on the other hand, happily plows through a scenario with little regard to where it comes from or where it's going. That has its advantages, though. Mark, being a college professor and natural nerd, is never at a loss for how to phrase things. But he tends to embellish, sometimes inserting too much literary texture (that's the poet in him coming through). Kym champions a more nonintrusive voice, constantly reminding Mark of the kinds of books we both like to read.

Above all else, we prefer escapism—mysteries by John Sanford, Sarah Peretsky, Greg Iles, and Val McDermid; thrillers by Preston and Child, of course, but also those by John Case, Andrew Klavan, Dan Brown, and Michael Crichton; warped fantasies (no dragons or elves) by Jonathan Carroll, Christopher Moore, Mario Acevedo, and Ramsey Campbell; sci-fi by Connie Willis, Charles Sheffield, Cordwainer Smith, John Barnes, Orson Scott Card, and Cory Doctorow. The lists could go on and on.

Okay, we do sometimes read something a little more highbrow. We like Laurie Wagner Buyer, Annie Proulx, Anita Diamant, Sara Gruen, Stacy Richter, Lorrie Moore. And yes, we even read the Pushcart Prize winners to keep our pulse on up-and-coming authors.

We read a lot because we think it helps our writing. And we're shameless when it comes to stealing techniques that impress us. John Case gave *The Genesis Code* a twist in the final sentence of the book. We liked it so well that we added a final-sentence twist to *The Silverville Swindle*—or we thought we had, until the editors read it. Days before our novel went to press, we ate lunch with the publishers to pitch them the sequel. When the conversation came back to the first book, they asked if we planned to reveal the hidden identity of one of the major characters. We thought we had through implied exposition along the way as well as in our final sentence. They didn't get it. We rushed home and rewrote the last two paragraphs and final sentence, making that character's identity unmistakable. It's a decision we've never regretted, and almost all of our readers tell us they didn't expect that ending. "Oh yeah," one reader told us, "there were hints throughout the book. I just didn't put it together until the end."

Here's a perfect example of what rigid writing can do to the quality of a story. We just knew the ambiguity at the end of *The Silverville Swindle* was enough to clue in our readers. We were wrong. We've been wrong about lots of things in our co-writing endeavors.

Several years ago, we wanted to tell an alternate history about Ankhsen-amun, the wife of King Tut. We read lots of books, did tons of research, and then sat down to outline the story arc. We wrote extensive summaries for twenty-two carefully crafted chapters, and thought to ourselves, "Man, this book is going to write itself!" While this may work for some writers, the strategy completely killed our passion for the project. We remained steadfast and followed our outline to every detail. By six chapters, we'd gotten pretty bored. We hadn't allowed the characters any voice in where the story was going. We all became miserable, and that manuscript still sits in a drawer at Chapter Six.

What's become more workable for us is to create a broad-stroke outline that gives us the flexibility to listen to our characters along the way. They may not always want to go where we had originally planned, and we've discovered we'd best listen to them.

We both tend to fall in love with those mouthy and opinionated characters, but we don't always relate to them in the same way. Take Denton Fine in *The Silverville Swindle*. He was a nice enough guy from the start—so nice we got bored with him. Originally, we'd tagged Denton as our protagonist, but he turned out to be a little too white-bread for our taste. Same with our real-life friends. If they're not quirky and eccentric, they don't make our lunch-date list for long.

Pleasance Pantiwycke, from *The Silverville Pantiwyckes*, on the other hand, always makes our A-list for lunch. She's a risk-taker and a slob, a black-marketeer and former female professional wrestler. Who wouldn't enjoy her conversation? It only took a few pages for her to take over the sequel and become our protagonist.

Switch gears to Skippy from our first novel. She's the only prominent female in the story, and one would think that Kym would empathize with her personality. Not so. Kym didn't like spending time with her at all. Getting inside a woman's head has always been more difficult for Kym, who finds it much easier to relate to men. Ironically, Mark got along with her just fine. This character serves as the main love interest for Billy, the story's protagonist. We talked at length about how far their intimacy should go and decided, in the end, that it wouldn't go far at all. Here's why: Several years ago, we'd bought a book on how to write erotica, hoping to make scads of money on the romance book wagon. We sat down and drafted out a torrid love scene, but it was simply too embarrassing to put into words. At least our words. "Love shaft" and "hot tunnel of passion" seemed like ridiculous and corny expressions that readers of the genre expected. We know it sells; we just couldn't do it. When it came to shaping the relationship between Skippy and Billy, we offered a lukewarm story arc, and our editors cried foul. Either consummate that relationship or back it off, they said. We backed off and left it up to the imagination of the readers. For two authors that insist that co-writing is like good sex, we still can't figure out why we can't pen erotica.

Billy, don't ask us why, turned into a protagonist that readers tend to like. We made him a cheat and a conman, and neither one of us really cared much for him. He was central, as the story unfolded, and we got stuck with him. He was also a cast member whose characteristics came from a sleazy guy we both knew years ago. We're not naming names, but he always used to hit on Kym. Which brings us to where we find our characters. Most are composites of personality types of people everyone knows: Grady, the curmudgeon rancher; Buford, the self-interested town promoter; Howard, the endearing village simpleton—all *Silverville Swindle* cast members. Maybe it's telling that we were most attached to Howard and easily crawled inside his head:

> *Howard liked to pedal. He didn't have to think about anything else—just push the right foot down and then push the left foot down. Sometimes he went so slow that his bike would wobble, but then he'd stand up on his pedals and pump until he sped up fast enough that it felt like flying.*
>
> *In some ways, it reminded him of massaging limbs. Whenever he helped Mr. Fine embalm bodies, Howard's job was to squeeze the arms and legs so the blood could come out and the embalming fluid could go in. At least, that's what Mr. Fine said it was for. First the right leg, and then the left leg. Just like pedaling.*

Howard looks at the world in a very simple way, one that makes sense to the child in all of us, and it was soothing to write from his perspective, taking everything at face value.

Buford *is* modeled after a specific person, but again we're not naming names. It's been interesting to us to watch our community try to guess his real identity.

Grady is another character we especially like. There's a little bit of all the ranchers we've ever known in him. Not too surprising since we've both lived in rural America most of our lives (Kym in Minnesota, South Dakota, and Montana; Mark in New Mexico; and both of us for the past twenty-plus years in western Colorado). So Grady's take on things was easy to capture. Right before the first *Silverville* hit local bookstores, we worried about how our neighbors would react to the way we portrayed the ranching lifestyle. But our daughter laughed at us, saying something like, "If a book doesn't have pictures, they're not going to read it!" She was joking, of course, but we bravely laughed along with her and waited for the novel to circulate. Several of our neighbors did read the book, and whew! they liked the way we'd described Grady. Kym had a real knack for capturing his style of speech, but she's always had a penchant for old ranchers. So Kym took the last word, literally, on what he said—and what he didn't.

Grady also rides a horse we know very well, 'Ole Moss. We modeled the mare after one we used to own named Belle. She was a bitch from the day she was born in our barn. At three weeks, she almost broke a neighbor's knee with a well-aimed kick, and when we turned her over to a professional trainer at age two, she charged her new teacher with bared teeth and flattened ears. We include in the story one of Belle's real antics when 'Ole Moss strikes out repeatedly at a hot wire fence once it shocks her. Belle would have been the perfect fit for Grady and she made it into our cast.

In the sequel, *The Silverville Pantiwyckes*, Mark took a shine to a character named Maurice LeVieux, a by-product who emerged from Mark's pretentious professor side, and Kym let him run with it. Maurice is the octogenarian arch nemesis of that story's protagonist, Pleasance. He's stuffy, pompous, and fastidious:

> *Maurice surveyed the row of tidily arranged ascots that filled the upper compartment of his suitcase. He selected one with just a blush of apricot to match his socks. He chuckled at his propitious talent to once again outmaneuver Pleasance. How careless of her to repeat Grady's name over the phone that fateful day he overheard her conversation. Poor child. Had she learned nothing from his example? By the time he had arranged to travel to Silverville, he already had Mr. O'Grady's phone number and address in his pocket.*
>
> *He adjusted the ascot, tucking it neatly inside his collar and around his papery throat. He sat on the bed and reached over to snap the garters to his socks.*

From the very beginning, we knew Maurice was going to be a fun character to work with. But you'll have to read the story to find out that he's not a typical anal-retentive guy. We hope he has quirks that catch readers off guard.

What caught *us* off guard was Cesar, a personality in our most recent screenplay. Created as an afterthought to complement the story's protagonist, Cesar pushed his way into the plot as one of the most colorful characters. It was creepy, like he was waiting in the wings for a casting call. Creepy because he possessed us both at the same time, with surprising flair that seemed to come from nowhere. Cesar really challenges our notion of where we thought characters originate. Even stranger, neither of us has ever *known* a Cesar. But there he was on the page. Here he's trying to convince his employer, Arlen (our protagonist) to go on a speed date:

> *Cesar smoothes down jet-black hair and straightens in his chair.*
> CESAR. If Cesar was in a stable full of women, he would prance like a stallion.
> JOY. I still say that's no way to meet a woman.
> CESAR. Don't listen to her, man.
> *Cesar turns toward Joy.*
> CESAR You see all the donuts in that box? People pick the tastiest ones. Arlen goes to a room full of women to pick the tastiest one.
> *Joy walks around the counter and comes over to sit at the table.*
> JOY. That's ridiculous. Arlen could get all kinds of diseases from the ones that he, uh, tastes.
> CESAR. Ah, but variety is the salsa of life.
> ARLEN. I don't know.
> CESAR. Why settle for a single flower when you can choose from a whole garden?
> *Cesar stands.*
> CESAR. Come! Come with me to my home, and I will teach you to dress and act so the ladies at your race date will lick your feet with desire.

We swear we didn't write this dialog; Cesar did. In fact, he just sort of grabbed the reins and ran with them. We often find that a particular character will determine the direction of a plot. Characters tell us what they need, what they have to say, and where they will and will not go. Unlike Cesar, most of our characters need fleshing out, and once we get to know them, we trust them to guide us to the end of the story. Our first novel took all sorts of twists and turns that we hadn't anticipated as the characters took on lives of their own. We almost felt like spectators rather than writers, our job merely to record what was going on in their universe.

Sometimes they even tell us what their names are. More often than not, surnames pop out about the same time a character shows up in a story. Last names occasionally stem from ones we've heard in our past or they'll relate to the personality—or just the opposite. In *The Silverville Swindle*, Howard Beacon isn't exactly a bright light; Billy Noble is anything but, whereas money preoccupies Buford Price. Same thing in *The Silverville Pantiwyckes*: Madame Pompeii is as disastrous as her namesake, Maurice LeVieux plays an old geezer ("LeVieux" is French for that), and the "three fools" are our hat tip to Moe, Larry, and Curly. Whether or not readers catch our wordplay, the name puns are amusing to us. In the screenplay excerpt above, we named our protagonist Arlen Starlin because it sounds funny, it's awkward to say, and it fits a person who encounters difficulties and uncertainties—in a black-comedy sort of way.

Arlen never had to live through a novel-life first; he and his playmates landed in a screenplay from the very start. Our new adventures in screenwriting have put a whole new spin on collaborative writing. We still follow the same techniques for telling a tale, but through the perspective of seeing the story on a big screen. We first gave it a shot with *The Silverville Swindle*, mostly because readers kept telling us the story would make a good movie. We've never let not knowing what we're doing stop us before—starting a magazine, putting out a weekly paper, writing that first novel—but this time it seemed like a good idea to find out more about how movie scripts come together.

The summer after the novel came out, we went to a writing conference that had a session on screenwriting. We decided to try it. That first draft taught us enough to know that our script was just that, a first draft. For one thing, we mostly cut-and-pasted dialog from the novel, and what we got turned into a monster, dialog-wise. Worse, when a film-maker read the script for us, he pointed out that one particular sentence would cost a studio ten thousand dollars. So back to the drawing board for us. We needed to think in terms of not only story but also production—and what kind of response we would get from future collaborators—i.e., producers, directors, and film companies. We buried our noses in books, subscribed to trade journals, and read successful scripts. Along the way, we learned a whole new approach to tightening up a story so that it fits inside two hours. And we discovered we really liked it.

No longer did we have to fill in so much background, and we could skip a lot of exposition altogether. We could completely focus on the key scenes; we both now looked at story as a series of visuals. Version 2.0 of *The Silverville Swindle* looks a lot different from the first draft, and very different from the novel. We chopped with gleeful abandon many peripheral characters and subplots completely disappeared and we repackaged conflict and action. We also rewrote the scenes to keep our protagonist in front of the camera. In the end, we think we created a tidy little package that won't cost a studio an arm and a leg. We must have done something right because it's gotten the attention of a Colorado-based independent film company. Time will tell where this one goes, but in the meantime, we're enjoying our new playground and have a few more screenwriting projects in the works. Not adaptations, but straight-to-script projects, like the one featuring Cesar and Arlen.

Will Arlen go on a speed date that leads to a hot rendezvous in bed? Probably not. Like we said before, we can't write love scenes. Our passion is private except when it comes to crafting a good tale together.

"We're still a sentence or two away from finishing this article," Kym says.

They stare at the screen, rereading the last paragraph, looking for any momentum they can use.

"Boy, I sure can't think of anything else to say." Mark sighs. "Can you?"

"Nope."

**Rosemerry Wahtola Trommer**, poet, writer, and organic fruit grower uses poetry to help people re-engage with the world beyond pagers and to-do lists. Trommer has authored and edited nine books and is widely anthologized. She is also a newspaper columnist, writes for magazines, teaches public speaking at Mesa State College, directs the Telluride Writers Guild, teaches writing in the public schools, and sings with a seven-woman *a cappella* group. Trommer was recently named Poet Laureate of San Miguel County.

# From Pretty Pink Bows to Chicken Manure: Embracing Poetry as Practice

### Rosemerry Wahtola Trommer

*"Things fall apart.
The center cannot hold."*
—William Butler Yeats, "The Second Coming"

THERE ARE EVENINGS we know, as if standing at the edge of an orchard in bloom on a night predicted to frost, that by the time we awaken, the world will not be the same.

It was one of those evenings. "I feel as if everything is breaking," I said.

Salida poet Jude Janett and I had been sitting in the front seat of my car in front of a coffee shop for an hour. I was crying. She was listening and nodding, sipping her signature latte, half caf, half decaf.

"Breaking open," she said at last. "Not down."

This is why I love words. Because they frame our experience. Because if we let them, two syllables and a new metaphor can make all the difference between interpreting an event as a catastrophe or a catalyst. Because things fall apart. And with words, we can break open a moment, and from there we can build it anew.

> I Have Found No Better Teaching
>
> than May's ripening apricots,
> rose cheeked and hail pocked,
> unsellable & sweetening anyway.

I live in a small white farmhouse on Colorado's western slope, surrounded by seventy acres of peaches, pears, apricots, nectarines, apples and cherries. After a year of commuting here with my son, I've finally nested in these trees, at least for the summer. I'm getting better at not knowing what comes next.

Alongside the orchard's green dominion snakes the muddy Gunnison River. The red sandstone cliffs of Dominguez Canyon dominate every horizon with their slowly eroding slopes. Tucked between cliffs hide small dunes of flesh-colored sand, gulches littered with volcanic rock and petrified wood, and walls pocked with barely visible rock art. Though the orchard itself feels abundant and fertile, all around us are reminders that everything transforms.

Four years ago, my husband Eric and I had looked at this property as a real estate investment. It was dramatic, remote, had plenty of water rights, and boasted three decrepit houses, a barn stuffed with trash, heaps of rusted cars, an inventory of unusable tractors and implements, and piles of dysfunctional irrigation parts. It was perfect.

This is my husband's specialty. He finds forlorn and fatigued properties and works with the land and infrastructure until it's revitalized. One drawback to the orchard: trees. Nearly twenty thousand fruit trees. Neither of us knew squat about growing fruit. We pulled back.

A year later, venture-less, our ignorance about growing fruit seemed less daunting. We could learn. We would hire a manager and continue to live in our home on the San Miguel River in Placerville, two hours south of the orchard.

That's how little we knew.

Our neighbor upstream on the Gunnison, a second-generation orchardist who had just passed his orchard on to his son, heard our plan to operate New Leaf Fruit remotely. He raised an eyebrow. He didn't say then, "We'll see about that." He saved his words until later. Until after my husband had moved there.

The move had been gradual. First Eric's clothes were gone from our bedroom closet. Then his tools vacated our garage. Then his computer left our office. It was months before I fully grasped the obvious. The orchard was not an investment; it was a total lifestyle change. Our summers would have nothing to do with climbing mountains knee-deep in lupine nor running rivers nor camping in snow-cradled alpine cirques. That was the old life. Summer's new activities involved hanging pheromone mating disruptors in apple and pear trees, fixing tractors, thinning apricots and repairing micro-sprinklers.

In the months leading up to the orchard purchase, Eric had worked on cleaning up the contract, researching water rights and untangling access issues—especially with the non-communicative Union Pacific. To get to the property, one must cross the tracks, and the rail bisects the orchard rows, its yellow engines carrying coal, scrap metal, sawdust and empty freight cars all hours of night and day. The railroad administration doesn't want to be reached and has constructed a nearly impenetrable wall around its higher ups. Eric was duly persistent, and in March 2007, we signed the dotted line.

Meanwhile, I'd researched the world of fruit, making contacts with other growers, soil scientists, marketers, packers, government officials and potential employees. I learned about organic certification and cultivation and how every grower does it differently. I learned why Colorado's peaches are sweeter than those from California—cold nights help. I learned it was as romantic as it sounded—making sweetness out of sunlight, water and soil. But, and like all successful romance, it takes a lot of work.

The research part suited me. As a writer and ex-journalist, I thrive on digging up facts, interviewing people and weaving the information into an understandable whole. I quickly learned there are no easy answers when it comes to growing fruit. For instance, how best to fertilize an acre of peaches? A foliar application of fish oil? Spread chicken manure? Plant dwarf white clover as a green manure? No two orchardists or scientists would give you the same answer. Amidst the ambiguity, however, everyone agrees on one point. If you are going to be a successful grower, you put growing first.

After visiting one of the region's most profitable, longstanding orchards, Eric and I drove home to Placerville together, sharing a rare toddler-free moment where we could actually listen and talk.

"What do you think?" he said. I knew he was referring not only to the Kropp's farm, but to the whole orchard proposition.

"It's not my dream." These were four of the scariest words I've ever said. I knew that Eric was increasingly excited about and invested in the purchase. And I knew I had better say something now so I didn't resent my silence later.

Miles of Paonia's leafless peach trees blurred by. Spring had yet to tease her greening fingers through their branches.

I tiptoed as much as I could with my voice, but my words were sledgehammers. "My dreams all revolve around words," I said. "My dreams revolve around writing, teaching and performing."

"I know," he said.

### Ars Poetica

*All wisdom is rooted in learning to call things by their right name.* —Confucius

Rain speaks many languages,
is fluent in tongues of abundance and scarcity.

Deranged by drought, I listen,
ears parched, nose lusty for the smell of rainbow.

No vocabulary rivals the certainty of rain
nor outshines the Buddha's best lecture:

two hours of silence
concluded by producing a single flower.

What language surpasses wisdom of petals?
Still, I thrill at the pleasure of naming,

the joy of verbs unfurling
from primitive places below the belly

before spiraling into the ear—
yes, here is the path of the poet:

to empty,
to listen,

to translate syntax of rain on bare limbs,
then sing with whatever words we have learned

and join our small voices
in the big conversation.

"Um, Dad," I said into the college dorm-room phone, "I'm not going to be a bio major anymore."

"That's fine," Dad said, even-toned. He's Finnish. Stoic.

"I want to be a poet. I'm going to be an English major."

The phone accumulated weight in my hand. Any words that might have wanted to be said buried themselves in our throats. I knew he would be disappointed. Having an MD for a daughter had long been his vision. And math and science were always my best subjects. But based on my present state of discontent with my lab courses, I speculated I would be unhappy in medical school, unhappy as an intern, then unhappy in my career. I was no William Carlos Williams. Every time we dissected, I fainted. Every time.

Dad cleared his throat. "Roxanne," he said, calling me by my childhood nickname, "Marry someone rich."

I first knew that I wanted to be a poet in fourth grade. Mr. Hendricks had given us an assignment to write about a color.

Being a predictable girl, I chose pink.

*Pink is pretty*
*and fingernail polish.*
*Lovely roses*
*I'd never abolish.*

I have always thought that writing is something I work at more than something that comes naturally to me. But what I learned in the composing of that first poem was that writing was fun. That I love to engage with words. That I love the sounds our tongues and teeth can make and the ways that two phonemes will resonate or clang with each other. That creating rhythm is addictive.

That first blush of a fourth-grade crush is what still draws me to poetry. It's a strong attraction to language—the reason I went on to earn a master's degree in English Language and Linguistics at the University of Wisconsin in Madison. I wanted to be intimate with syntax and phonology, to know the rules of our language as well as I know the names of the native plants (and weeds) that grow in my backyard.

Though I loved the education, I was miserable much of my graduate school career. I found the English department to be closed-door and competitive. With so little money at stake, what was left to vie for was ego. I was not a department darling. In fact, I was an annoyance. I wanted to blend concentrations, to study both literature and linguistics and marry the two, but the departments were on two floors with two separate administrations. I didn't fit in either camp, and neither camp wanted me.

The decision to leave higher education came as a result of one of my favorite phone calls ever with my father. After the initial English major shock, he and my mother stepped in to support me as a poet. They were then, and still are, my biggest cheerleaders. In fact, Dad even created a cheer for me that he makes me recite with him whenever I need a boost: *One, Two, Three, Yeaaaaaah Rox!*

But for this particular phone call, the name of the game was *no*. No more school. For nearly two years, I cried every day, sometimes two or three times a day. Depleted of energy and enthusiasm, I wanted out. But it was hard for me to relinquish the doctorate. I'd thought being a professor would be the perfect complement to being a poet. And if I didn't do that, what would I do?

"Just say no," Dad said on the other end of the line.

"No," I whimpered.

"That was wimpy," he said. "Say NO!"

"No." I said, a bit louder.

"No!" he shouted.

"No!" I roared. Until the two of us were bellowing full choruses of "No! No! No!"

The "no" session was therapeutic and effective. I felt released from the walls I'd built around myself—ivory towers of shoulds and expectations.

Though these days, I think I might have handled it with a yes.

In 2006, I was teaching for the Aesthetic Education Institute of Colorado and worked with Colorado Springs theater artist Birgitta Dupree. She taught me a story game called *Yes, And?* Once again, two syllables created a new window through which I could better see the world.

The game needs two people. The first supplies an opening line. For instance, "Once upon a time there was a woman." The next player says, "Yes, and she was ____," filling in the blank with whatever comes to mind. Player one responds, "Yes, and …" The two players continue to tell a story, volleying the action back and forth, each time beginning their turn with the words "yes, and."

I use this technique with myself every day. There's so much I've tried to say no to. No to feelings, because they are uncomfortable. No to anger, no to messiness, no to moving away from Placerville, no to redefining my dreams.

By confronting each awkward situation with *yes, and*, I move myself forward. *Yes* is the only word that makes sense. It acknowledges that what is *is* what is. Yes, my husband moved away. Yes, I am pregnant again (surprise!). Yes, my son has colic and cries incessantly. Yes, my poetry manuscript was rejected by Ghost Road Press. Yes is not a threat. It is a willingness to see the world with all its warts and difficulties.

The secret to dealing with the consequences of yes is the next word: *and*. I easily trap myself in dualities, embracing an "or-based" world: right or wrong, good or bad, black or white.

*And* is how the world really works. An action might be right and wrong. Things are often simultaneously good and bad. The world is full of wishy-washy gray. *And* leads us into whatever comes next—reconciliation, parenthood, moving to an orchard, or a meal full of saturated fat and all its consequences.

Out of the *yes, and* discovery came my poetry collection, *Suitcase of Yeses*, poems inspired by the idea that if we want to walk more joyfully through life, we might as well say yes to it all.

And.

## Yes, And

Last night the poet said the heart is full
    of sea water.
And I say yes, with tides
    and weeds and things that sting.
And I seem to have lost
    my raft, where did it go?
because I'm too, too tired to swim.
    And, I say, the heart is full
of this spring rain, the kind that clings
    to bare branched aspen trees
and mutinies of filaree that green beneath the feet.
    And the heart is full of puddles
Far too deep to properly wade with shoes.
    Best to muddle in barefoot,
naked heel, tender toe,
    with the un-soled arch that holds the weight
of so much fullness, so much ache.
    I know I go on loving you
like water.

During those two years studying the science of English on the isthmus between lakes Mendota and Monona, one of my biggest lessons was in geography. I learned Colorado was my home. Ever since I was ten years old, I'd lived in the foothills of the Rockies above Golden. Ponderosa forests and gray rock fields above tree line were the landscapes that defined my joy.

After every summer visit to my parents, I would cry as the foothills disappeared in the rearview mirror of my blue Subaru. By the time I got to the Kansas border, I'd pull over beside the sunflower fields and have a nose-running, eye-swelling cry. The host of brown and orange heads would affirm my grief, bobbing up and down as if to say, "Yes, your roots are here. Don't worry. You'll return."

### Couldn't We All Use a Miracle?

Above tree line the heart can breathe.
At last, a space that does not try to contain it,
a landscape sufficiently vast for love and love and love
and oh, says the heart, at last you get it,
the map is only a rendering,
and the pleasure is in the wandering
and the miracle is in the noticing.

When I did return to Colorado in 1994, it was to Telluride. There, in a town of less than two thousand at the end of a dead-end road, I met Art Goodtimes, a renowned Colorado performance poet. He took me on as a stringer for the *Telluride Times-Journal* and offered to co-teach a poetry class with me for the local Ah Haa School for the Arts.

Though my title was teacher, I was Art's student. My poetic background was academic and critique-oriented. I wanted people to print their poems and hand them around for red-penciling. Art, on the other hand, thrilled in the oral presentation of poems. He wanted poems read aloud. "We've lost the art of listening," he would say. And trying to follow the spoken poems of our students, I found he was right. Without a page in front of me and a pen in my hand, I couldn't follow what was being said.

The practice of sitting in a circle and listening to poems became like prayer for me. It hastened me back to my original love of language—cadence and resonance. There was a freeing lack of judgment—the poems weren't meant to be dissected, they were to be experienced. And it ushered me into a new kind of poetic community—one that was based on support of each other's voices. In a classroom there are limited seats. In a book, there are limited pages. In a department, there are limited jobs. But a circle of readers and listeners can always adjust its circumference.

In part because of Art, my poetic circles widened. Stylistically, he encouraged me to "break open" my writing. Let it get messier, he'd say, less linear, more guttural. He still teases me about how tightly wound my work can be. A recent poem I sent him about surrender was written in strict meter and rhyme. The irony was not lost on Art. He pointed it out, adding, "I hope I can help just a bit to free the wild hyena hiding in the chrysanthemums."

My circles also widened in terms of people I met. Art recommended I be included in an anthology edited by then Crested Butte resident David Rothman, *Geography of Hope: Poets of Colorado's Western Slope*. The poets in that book, including Luis Lopez, Karen Chamberlain, Jim Tipton, Mark Todd and Bruce Berger, enthusiastically volunteered to read around the state. I thrilled in my place in this new community, traveling and reading and meeting other folks who loved words and this landscape of mountain, river, desert and cirque.

Being part of a collection focused on place helped me define my attraction to writing. I became increasingly conscious of the relationships between exterior landscapes and inner, emotional landscapes. How finding a wild rose bush rising from a rock mirrored my own sense of personal possibility—a willingness to bloom despite adverse conditions. How the way mullein seeds replant themselves in a field mirrors the way seeds of jealousy multiply in our minds.

Landscape. Language. Listening. Yes. And lots of hard work.

Put Me In My Place

*If nothing delights us, we get mean.* —Jan Worth

> I come to this alpine meadow for kisses,
> how dew does what dew does
> with soft morning lips.
> I'd walk thirty miles for this,

> this damp green communion
> beneath aspen dapple
> where larkspur spark violet
> above white lace umbels.
>
> This is what a body is for,
> to be dwarfed by beauty,
> to give itself up to a day with no wind
> and a bath of dawn light.
>
> And this is why legs learn quickly to clamber,
> this is why lungs learn to love the burn.
> Because petals unfurl.
> Because dew disappears.

Another reason I am drawn to writing is an insatiable appetite for beauty. I am willing to find it everywhere, not that it's hard in the San Juan Mountains or the Gunnison River Canyon to notice what is lovely. So often do I blurt out, "Oh, isn't that beautiful," that my son Finn, at age three, already points out to me the radiant frost on the trees after dawn or the pale yellow prickly pear flowers hiding behind the sage and says, "Oh Mommy, isn't it be-YOU-tee-ful?"

Though beauty is always to be found, I am not always available to it. I am governed by a strong Protestant work ethic and obsessed with accomplishment and efficiency. My to-do lists are long and I thrill in checking them off. I multi-task everything—just today I simultaneously brushed my teeth, made the bed and listened to phone messages so that I would be able to do nothing but play for an hour when my son woke up.

Everything in its place. My spice rack is alphabetized. My bookshelves are ordered by subject. In a field of purple penstemon and native grass, I fixate on weeds. At our six acres in Placerville, I have spent whole summers uprooting sweet clover, dandelions, bull thistle, cheat grass, black medic and salsify. By hand.

In my efforts to put the field "right," I often forget to look up and notice slant light on red cliffs, to follow the hummingbird's flight toward the garden sunflowers, to smell the lush dank of the San Miguel River.

I get what I call the "busy blinders," imaginary shields that allow me to only see whatever weed comes next.

I often recite for myself a quote from the Mad Hatter who says to Alice, "You're not paying attention. And if you don't pay him, you know he won't perform."

### In Search of Buried Treasure

We didn't go looking for treasure. In fact, we were going for a walk.

But after three steps into evergreen shade,
>he drops to his knees and begins to furrow.
>>*It's here, mama*, he says. *Let's dig.*

I pick up a knobby spruce twig and poke absently at dirt,
>hoping we can start walking again.
>>*No, mama, like this. With your hands.*

I pretend I don't hear.

He takes my hands in his own, forces them down.
>Fine sand runs through my fingers,
>>old spruce needles swim in it like commas unstrung
>>>from sentences.

I settle in, sifting and digging up dirt. Making piles.
>No mama, deeper than that, he says,
>>scratching with his nails into the hardpan.

I dig deeper, past my desire to keep my hands clean.
>Past whatever I had set out to do. Treasure is cold
>>and filled with crooked things that slip through fingers.

I suppose in most jurisdictions, what Finn and I found in the duff wouldn't qualify as treasure: "a concentration of riches, often one which is considered lost or forgotten until being rediscovered."

But dig beneath the surface of the word and find it comes from the Greek, *thesaurus*, the root of our cognate, meaning "a treasury of words."

As a verb, *to treasure* implies we "accumulate and store away, as for future use."

But what I learned on that otherly-fated walk was the opposite. That treasure is in the moment. It's in the letting go. Of the future. Of our own plans. Of what we think we want.

Letting go has been the theme of most of my recent poems. It's as if the poems are proofs for me as I try to learn these new geometries of family and place. I'm trying to learn what all treasure hunters know: clues are everywhere. I just need to be willing to notice, to see beneath the tarnish of expectation. Treasure might just look like sitting with my husband on an old farmhouse porch, watching the full moon rise above the tops of the peach trees.

> In Twenty Years You Might Forget
>
> how warm this morning greeted you
> despite its thin gray coverlet.
> How reason kept on sleeping, despite
>
> the brash occasion of geese
> that surprised the dawn, how they flayed
> their wings on the scrim of wakening
>
> before unsettling knee-high weaves of grass.
> How the Russian olive spread sweetness in the room.
> Even peach trees seem attentive today,
>
> their leaves lance-splayed like emerald praise,
> like a chorus of green hoorahs, full and demanding
> your attention. And how, for this moment, you remembered
>
> to give it.

Why poetry? Why not essays or fiction or how-to manuals?

Control.

Considering my delight in a well-kempt field and an orderly spice cabinet, it's no surprise, perhaps, that I'm a devotee of meter and rhyme. For my English thesis at Colorado College, I wrote a ninety-three page paper on Gerard Manley Hopkins, teasing apart his sonnets to understand his complex use of rhythm and sound. I suppose it's the scientist in me that loves these structures and rules—the part of me that would have excelled in medicine if only I could have kept from passing out at the dissections.

Though my present poem-a-day practice is most often free verse, I've written many dozens of sonnets, triolets, villanelles and glosses. That passion for resonance and tempo informs everything else I write. I hear poems more than read them. I take comfort in the advice I once read from Auden: If given a choice between a word that makes more sense or a word that sounds better, choose the one that sounds better. As he would say, "The sound of words is inseparable from their meaning." I love finding advice that reinforces my own opinion.

I also enjoy an interview on Poets in Person with James Merrill, in which he speaks of formal poetry as a metaphorical house that he can inhabit. "I would never want to build my own house," he says, but in choosing to use a received form, we let someone else build the "walls of the house" and we bring to the interior our own creative sensibility. It's the essence of chaos theory: in a finite space there is room for infinite complexity.

I'm like Merrill in that I enjoy receiving a space, then seeing what I might do to make it my own. A form gives the sense that there is a pervasive order to things. I like that. And to parse our language into iambs, to discover rhymes that allow the ear to nod—this is to push poetry to its edges and see what it can do. Or to ruin it.

It's a heady sense of control and satisfaction to come up with a sonnet finely rendered that also makes the head nod—especially if my subject is one that makes me feel helpless, vulnerable or at odds.

### At Peggy's Memorial

And as they tried to nail her down inside
a box of frozen words, I tried to find
her in the swirl of blue stained glass behind
the altar, wondering where she might hide
her laugh amidst the mourners here. I tried
to find her in the sprightly hymns. The mind
desires a tight container, wants some kind
of sealed frame where death is codified.

> But grief escapes, as does the soul. It sneaks
> like sunshine through opaque blue glass. We might
> conspire to clasp it in our hands. It leaks.
> We seize. It seeps. We knit our fingers tight
> around what never can be grasped. It streaks
> through every crack. Our hold on life, how light.

Though I think it serves me to be diligent in my pursuit of "just the right word," the downfall can be retentive poems, dull at their best and didactic at their worst. Poems that try to contain things then tie them up with pretty pink bows and leave no room for mystery. This is poetry as product.

For many years, I've been a pretty pink bow tier. I've used poems as boxes, as ways to rectify a messy world in the same way that I try to rid the field of weeds—imposing sense and order on something given to chaos or complexity. With poems, I can create little prisons for things that make me uncomfortable, banish them to the page, then hide them away.

That's shifted. Perhaps because I'm older. Perhaps because containment didn't work. Perhaps it's reading Rumi. Maybe motherhood. Whatever the reasons, I'm increasingly interested in digging in the muck, kissing disorder, using poetry to open windows instead of closing doors. Driving this new poetic approach is a poem-a-day ritual that I've observed more on than off for the last three years.

I've struggled many years with blank page blues, unwilling to write anything for the risk that it not be perfect. But writing a poem a day, I accept not every poem will be a masterpiece. It frees me to write more open poems, to embrace poetry not as product but as a practice.

There's a lovely side effect. Sometimes masterpieces come. As Billy Collins once said, "Sit in an aviary long enough and sooner or later a bird will sit on your head." And a lot of them poop on my feet. Fine. Call it compost for growing a garden of yeses.

And. Some things stay the same. My spice cabinet still begins with Allspice, Arrowroot, Basil, Cinnamon, Cloves …

> *Producing order out of chaos involves a change in the system, which can only be produced by expending energy. The expenditure of energy is never perfectly efficient and so it always increases the overall amount of energy that is irretrievably disordered, even as order is produced from the remaining energy.* —Richard Carrier, "Entropy Explained"

If poetry has been my prayer in learning to surrender, then running the orchard is a seventy-acre advanced degree. Sure, we can decide whether to plant our cherries on Mazzard or Gisela 6 rootstock. We can choose to use concentrated vinegar instead of hoes to control bindweed. But we can't control frost. And we can't control late season hail. And when four thousand new peach trees start to die, it does no good to point fingers. It matters only that we evaluate what is and then determine our next step.

And that is, I suppose, how I find myself here on Colorado's western edge, still writing a poem a day, but for now embracing motherhood, marriage and cultivation instead of poetry residencies and literary festival organization.

It was not my dream to be a fruit grower. But dreams are ephemeral and life is now. And now. When I finally realized that my now no longer included my life partner, it wasn't a now I wanted to inhabit, no matter how beautiful the mountains surrounding now were.

When writing a poem, sometimes I think I know the end before I start. Sometimes I try to steer the poem in a certain way toward a certain truth or discovery. These poems seldom succeed. As my friend, Denver poet Kathryn Bass says preconceived endings are a kind of "emergency exit" that we create so that we might eject ourselves from the poem before the poem is necessarily ready to let us out.

I'm glad I didn't press eject. In embracing this new kind of Colorado life where the days are measured by the color of the fruit—even now we're in the ruby stage of cherries that precedes the deep mahogany of full maturity—I've found that I'm breaking again. Open. Not down.

And lucky for me, the poems don't care where we live.

## Ohm or Om

I have tried to resist the killing frost,
to create enough heat in my defiance
to save a whole orchard of pear and peach.
As if worry could raise a May night one degree.

I invent new battle hymns in my blood.
With my friction, I try to protect the trees.
But fervor has no effect on freeze,
does not defend what browns.

The night has its way with me.
Surrender becomes my name.
Before we understand acceptance,
we must refuse to believe what is,

must wrestle with every bit of our lattice
the tide of blind inheritance
until all our nos are replaced by oms
and hum is the only law that sticks,

till we bow to the current ecstasy,
widen the scope, increase the flow,
become the rare conductor
who knows how to let go.

**Larry Meredith** has been a writer all his working life. A journalist, public relations director, and freelancer, he has written thousands of news stories, press releases, magazine articles, video scripts, and newspaper columns.

He is the author of the historical novel *This Cursed Valley*, a Spur Award finalist from the Western Writers of America, and has a second novel in the hands of a literary agent. He has written three screenplays, and was recently selected as a "Colorado Voice" by the *Denver Post*.

Meredith recently retired from his position as Assistant to the President and Director of Public Relations for Western State University in Gunnison, Colorado. His varied career has included stints as Public Relations Director and Director of Instructional Technology for two Kansas colleges; owner for twenty years of Innovative Communications Corporation, a public relations, video production, and marketing firm; a newspaper reporter and editor; an advertising and sales promotion executive for a Fortune 500 company.

# The Writing Life: Fraught with Monsters, Real and Imagined

## Larry Meredith

WITH ALL THE wonderful and exciting professions from which to choose, why would a young person with any spunk, drive, intelligence, verve, ambition, or just plain old common horse sense want to become a writer? After all, as Alan Furst says, it's a life in which "you sit alone in a room and fight the language."

Thank God there are those who would rather wrestle with words than design bridges or create actuarial tables or plot missile trajectories or calculate the inevitability of an asteroid plummeting into the Earth at the precise moment of the autumnal equinox on the Salisbury Plain.

Of course we need bridges to get across the river to our jobs and all that other stuff, too. But, just as importantly, we need wordsmiths, fashioners of exquisite sentences, bunches of which laid end-to-end can bring to anxious readers endless joy, fuller understanding, an itch to know more, a surge of emotion, a pang of fear, a sense of sudden recognition, relief that there are others who have the same problems, escape.

But, still, why? Why would one want to endure the agony of going through the excruciatingly painful processes required of the writing life before reaching an uncertain end that is, always and ultimately, fraught with monsters real and imagined?

For one young man it began with the discovery of a book on a shelf in a small school library deep in the heart of rural Kansas, not far from where Superman fell to earth as an infant and just across the pasture from Dorothy and Toto's farm.

As he walked the high school halls from class to class the young man cupped his hand around the spine of the book and kept the cover against his leg or stomach lest football buddies discover he was reading something called *The Royal Road to Romance*. This, however, was not a book that would be among those labeled "Romance Novels" on the shelves at Borders book stores. This was Richard Halliburton's first book, written in 1925, in which he describes how, upon his graduation from Princeton, he decided to eschew a life of business and career for one of "romance," journeying to far-off lands. Who could resist the following?

> I hungered for the romance of great mountains. From childhood I had dreamed of climbing Fujiyama and the Matterhorn, and had planned to charge Mount Olympus in order to visit the gods that dwelled there. I wanted to swim the Hellespont … float down the Nile in a butterfly boat, make love to a pale Kashmiri maiden beside the Shalimar, dance to the castanets of Granada gypsies, commune in solitude with the moonlit Taj Mahal, hunt tigers in a Bengal jungle—try everything once.

Great Scott, good grief, and glory be! Could anything be more wonderful?

This particular young man had thought he would become a dentist.

Now, however, and pardon the pun, he had found something he could sink his teeth into and get excited about and have fun while he was at it, too.

So he went into journalism.

You laugh!

Since then the young man, now no longer young but unwilling to consider himself old, has traveled the country and the world. He has journeyed along the southern edge of the Gobi Desert and touched the far western end of China's Great Wall. He has kissed a beautiful lady in a gondola as they plied the canals of Venice, stood amid crashing waves at Land's End in southwestern England, visited Pompeii and the Acropolis and Mayan ruins and other wonders of the world.

And yet, he chose to set first novel in Colorado.

Let me explain.

Like many of you, I dreamed at an early age of someday writing a novel. It would be a big novel, not a tiny thin-spined tome but a hefty brick-like book that would weigh as heavily in the mind as in the hand.

But I understood that one must first learn the trade. So I wrote for newspapers and I wrote press releases, video scripts, magazine articles and advertising. Everything but a novel.

Did I really want to be a writer? What did I have to say? Was whatever I might ultimately say worth the energy demanded of me? Or did I mainly want to have written and be read? F. Scott Fitzgerald said, "You don't write because you want to say something; you write because you've got something to say."

I decided I had something to say and, therefore, would write. Maybe I rationalized this unreasonable decision based on a theory posed by Furst, who believes that "writers don't actually want to write books, they want to read them, but, discovering that they are unavailable to be read, because they are unwritten, they write them."

There were many unwritten books I longed to read. So which one would I write? What would I choose as a topic? My world was wide, I thought, the possibilities endless. China's Yellow River, England's Cotswolds, Mexico's Chichen Itza, the tiny Greek island of Santorini, the rigorous Chilkoot Pass route to the Yukon gold fields.

Then why Colorado?

The red-rocked point looms over the central Colorado valley like a monster ship's prow. It towers protectively above a silver thread of river that drains a mystical land teeming with the history of the American West.

A man sits on his small porch and studies the perpendicular cliffs of the butte, which are framed by soaring branches of slender cottonwood trees. The joyful cries of his children playing in the vacant land next door are muffled by thoughts of Ute Indians and the tiny *ini'pute* thought by the Utes to inhabit the point and to play a crucial role in the perpetuation of "the curse."

There are beguiling stories of the legend of the curse, believed to have been placed on the valley by a Ute holy man in 1879 as he and his band were being driven by the U.S. military to reservations in the southwestern part of the state. There are stories of ghosts and spirits and tiny beings that Ute legends say have some control over the destiny of the valley. Old timers speak with a mixture of sadness and pride of the history of explorers, trappers, prospectors, miners and others who have attempted to use the valley and its resources to their own ends. They shake their heads as they talk of early successes in the valley, the upshot of which, in most cases, was inevitable failure.

Is the curse real?

That question was the basis for research that resulted in my historical novel, *This Cursed Valley*.

I was interested in the curse, of course, its genesis and whether or not it had been effective in denying the white man the benefits of this valley that the Utes had inhabited throughout their existence in Colorado's Rocky Mountains.

What I found was a story not unlike those of hundreds of other locations throughout the West during the last decades of the nineteenth century and into the twentieth. The history of this valley mirrored that of the rest of the interior West so well, I believed, that it offered an opportunity to tell that history within the confines of one isolated valley.

The thing that would make it different was "the curse." That and the fact it would be a uniquely Colorado story. An historical Colorado novel. A "brick" of a novel.

Some may question the wisdom of spending such a great deal of time on another story of the West. It's all been said, we know the history, we'd rather read something new.

The cliché states unequivocally "that there's nothing new under the sun." We all know, however, that what is important is the way in which old stories are told anew. How can a writer make a familiar story new and different? I believe it is by creating unique characters that inhabit those oft-told tales of wars historic and recent, stories of the end of innocence, of love lost and found again, of justice triumphing over evil, of the search for God, of every human endeavor whether historic, current, or in some fantasy world far in the future.

During a conversation about good writing, in this case especially in terms of writing for the silver screen, fifty-three-year film veteran Ted Bayouth (his screen name is Ted White) said "a good screenplay is simply a well-written story about interesting people doing interesting things." What works in one genre, I believe, must surely work in another. *Interesting people doing interesting things.* Let me add—in an interesting setting and during an interesting time.

*Interesting people doing interesting things.* People tackle problems in their own way. The success they celebrate or the failure they suffer is the stuff of which stories are made. Consider your daily or weekly newspaper. Why do so many of its pages carry less "news" and more "features" on *interesting people doing interesting things*? Maybe it's because the "news" is often so depressing that readers more and more often turn to the feature articles to find stories of, yes, *interesting people* who have found new methods of accomplishing old goals, who have withstood adversity and emerged triumphant, whose problems are worse than our own.

I decided I could incorporate some or all of those themes into a story that was set in the West. I wanted to write about the West, by darn, and so I would. Even if the story has been told before. And told again. And again.

Wallace Stegner, that late great writer of essays, stories and novels, most of which are set in the West and deal with Western themes, found newness in almost every aspect of the West. In an essay called "The Rocky Mountain West" he wrote: "The West is still nascent, still forming, and that is where much of its excitement comes from. It has a shine on it, it isn't tired."

What is interesting to any individual writer, I believe, will be of interest to others. Written well, peopled with strong characters and offering new insights into the topic, a story is worth the effort put into it. In fiction, "story" is the key, whether historical, contemporary, or set in the future. Story, story, story. Interesting people. Realistic people dealing with realistic problems. Story. Well-developed characters. Good writing. Situations readers can relate to in their own lives. And, of course, story.

Over a long period of time I researched the history of the West and of the specific valley that was the setting for my novel. At the same time I mulled over the storyline and the people who would bundle it all together and make it meaningful and interesting. Finally, in an astonishing burst of energy (actually, over a period of a few years) I created a twelve-hundred page manuscript into which, I now realize, I had poured almost every bit of information I had learned. Some of it, I now know, had little to do with "the story."

I quickly realized I must become my own editor. After many pared-down versions, painful tightening, excruciating deletions, and frankly joyful re-writing, I created a manuscript that Pearl Street Publishing of Denver found suitable and published as a 566-page novel.

Here's the point of all that.

Some stories take years to germinate and then to slowly find a life, a direction, an essence of their own that can take more years to fully bloom and become real and solid and meaningful to someone other than the writer. As Doris Lessing says, "In the writing process, the more a thing cooks, the better." Others agree that there is value in a long process of imagining. In a letter to Willa Cather, Sarah Orne Jewett wrote, "The thing that teases the mind over and over for years, and at last gets itself put down rightly on paper—whether little or great, it belongs to Literature."

Of course, as I learned quickly, a writer must produce other work while patiently waiting for the right time to begin writing the piece that has slowly cooked somewhere in the recesses of his or her mind. One must continue to write. But we all know that.

Here's another literary thought from Vladimir Nabokov: "Caress the detail, the divine detail."

Or, as another writer friend once said to me: "Facts are eloquent."

If you do sloppy research, your readers will tell you about it. While many writers find research tedious, I find it one of the more enjoyable parts of the writing process. The wonders of the past intrigue me and, for a writer of historical fiction, getting the past right is paramount. For a writer dealing with any period of time, any subject, it's important to get it right.

Don Coldsmith, a Kansan and a prodigious writer of historical fiction (see the *Spanish Bit* series and other books of his—there are more than six million in print) preached the importance of careful research. Someone will always catch your errors, he said, whether you refer to a dress style that hadn't been created at the time of your story, a rifle that was yet to be designed, a phrase that was not yet in vogue, or even a whistling teakettle that doesn't belong in the story.

Don read an early draft of *This Cursed Valley* and jumped all over my whistling tea kettle reference, telling me they weren't invented until a few years after the time one appeared in that draft of my manuscript. How in the world would someone know that? The fact that he did speaks to the careful research he has done over the years and the value he places on accuracy.

Here's a story that also relates to accuracy—not so much the writer's but in this case, the editor's.

In 2007—an eternity ago based on news cycle time—I wrote a column for the *Denver Post* that seemed to have nothing to do with the craft of writing. In a short time, however, I discovered it provided insights into wordsmithing that in hindsight all writers think they instinctively know, but too often ignore or forget.

The column explained that drivers on Colorado's Western Slope roads in the spring and fall often encounter herds of cattle being driven to or from the high country. "Inevitably," I wrote, "the residue of their passing is readily apparent." Not long before writing the column, I had read a letter to the editor in an area newspaper from a woman I suspect was a part-time resident who complained about the resulting smell and the mess it left on her car. I suggested that the smell doesn't linger, and vehicles can be washed.

"The odor," I wrote, "has the smell of history in it. The complaining letter's scent reflects some of today's reality on the Western Slope. Neither is especially bad."

The title I suggested for the column was: "Defined by Cow Poop on the Road." When it was published, however, the headline was "Defined by Road Apples."

Well shoot, every self-respecting Westerner knows that road apples are left by *horses*, and that cattle leave cow patties.

The point: never assume that your readers (or your editors) have a base of knowledge sufficient to discern esoteric meaning from a phrase or a page you believe should be perfectly clear to anyone brilliant enough to want to read what you have written. My column had been targeted at those Colorado West Slopers who would appreciate the lack of understanding among newcomers about how things work over here. The fact that it would first be scrutinized by a big city editor was of less concern to me than meeting the deadline for submission.

The column also dealt with the concept of change and how newcomers are part of the reason for the changes, good and not so good, which much of the mountain West is undergoing. The reaction to this one individual column has been instructive in terms of how readers interpret an author's words. It is also quite interesting how a writer's main point can get lost thanks to one errant turn of phrase. Most of the reaction was to blame me (and not the headline writer) for using the term "road apples." I know I should simply be glad somebody read it. I hope many of those who read the column but did not respond via email, phone or letter, did get it.

I thought I had done a relatively good job, in less than seven hundred words, of making points about change. For example: "Thanks to technology, the world's business can often be as easily transacted from Gunnison as from Denver. That fact alone has transformed the West Slope from a secluded, snow-covered headwaters region into an accessible snow-covered headquarters for business and commerce of all kinds."

And, later: "The barber shop of the past is now an antique store. Yesterday's carriage shop has become a trendy coffee shop or a boutique stocked with exotic and rare perfumes and a gaggle of doodads that appeal to all of us. There's nothing wrong with that. Businesses emerge to meet demands."

I often wonder about the woman I mentioned who wrote the letter to the editor. If she read my column, did she recognize herself or did the concept of change mean much to her? Does she, indeed, realize that she, and others like her, are the agents of that change? If she did understand her role in the changing West, she might not have given a hoot, wishing it would change even more and that those smelly cows would stay off the road. On the other hand, assuming she didn't see herself as a catalyst for change, she was probably not a part of the audience I hoped to reach with my column.

The point: know your audience and write your brains out to convince them, to mollify them, to upset, engage, enrage, excite or even disgust them. Have a goal. Don't worry about the potential readers who will never "get it" and concentrate instead on those whom you have a chance to reach.

As I wrote that particular column, I had to agree with myself that newcomers are often more apt to attempt to inflict their personal preferences relating to quality of life issues on the old timers rather than trying hard to adapt to the culture of the land to which they are immigrating. I also had to admit that I was among the relative newcomers to the valley where I now make my home. Despite owning Colorado property for decades, I had not been a permanent resident there and thus became, and forever will be, a newcomer.

I consider myself a Coloradan, though, and am pleased to be included in this collection of essays by Colorado writers. I take the sobriquet seriously, and proudly. My Colorado novel, however, was written while I lived in Kansas, a state that once was considered part of the West, later as a Midwestern state and even more recently as one of the plains states. So I moved to Colorado and wrote a novel set in Kansas. And, despite the declaration by the "Center of the American West" at the University of Colorado at Boulder that the "New West" begins at the foothills of the Rocky Mountains (and excludes California), my Kansas novel, set in contemporary times, deals with themes common to the American West. Even though the Center's *Atlas of the New West* points out that "the 'West' keeps moving around in time and space," Kansas will, in my mind, always be a part of the old West, no matter where contemporary demographers place it in modern America.

My novel, *McKee's Ocean*, deals with themes that are common to the

West and features people who, though living in today's turbulent times, might well have lived a hundred years ago and, if so, would have met the same kinds of problems with the same thoughtfulness and determination to separate wrong from right.

I hope you can sense my passion for writing about the West and western issues. They are universal issues and should resonate with all people who recognize that our problems are their problems, that western America is playing a larger role than ever before in domestic politics and the global economy. Yes, there is much yet to be written about the West. And, even though some continue to take thoughtless approaches to dealing with Western issues such as water, minerals and open space, it's hard to be pessimistic about this part of the country. After all, as Stegner says, "This is where optimism was born."

I'm optimistic that even though some publishers turn up their noses at anything smelling even slightly "western," good books set in the West that deal with important Western themes will reach bookshelves. I'm optimistic that readers will want to know more about the West, not necessarily about the mythic West that everyone thinks they know, but about Stegner's West—this land of little rain and big consequence, of great expectations and unlimited opportunity. I'm optimistic that the novel I'm working on now (set in the West, naturally) will find an enthusiastic publisher. I'm just as optimistic that at least one of the three screenplays I've written might actually be produced.

*Camera pan from mountain to sky, fade to black. Fade up on a new topic.*

Speaking of screenwriting, let's talk for a moment about the difficulties in moving from one genre to another. Short story writers, poets and journalists understand the need for brevity, clarity, and concise descriptions that paint word pictures so vividly that readers quickly grasp meaning, metaphorical concepts and environmental relationships. Novelists can take longer to describe, explain, create interesting dialogue and choreograph action scenes.

If you are a screenwriter, or have aspirations of becoming one, you will face problems akin to those bedeviling the short story writer or the poet. Consider, for example, the daunting task of adapting a three hundred-and-fifty to four hundred page novel into a typical 120-page screenplay. That's the equivalent of a two-hour movie—basically one page per minute of screen time. The task is made easier, of course, in that vivid scenic descriptions, for example, are unnecessary because the camera takes care of that task. Still, enough (but not too much) exposition must get the viewer quickly into the story, dialogue must be pared, and the writer can't let the story drag or viewers will take that opportunity to go get more popcorn or to find the restroom.

As a novelist, I have benefited significantly from my time as a journalist, just as I have learned a great deal from short story writers, poets and screenwriters. I believe journalism is a wonderful background for a writer, no matter where his or her interests lie. Journalists must learn to write clearly (so those readers with the ability level of an eighth grader can understand), quickly (to meet stringent deadlines), and sparely (due to limited space in newspapers or magazines). They must also be interested in doing the required research so their stories are factual and believable. Sounds to me like the makings of a fine writer of books (fiction or non-fiction), of collections of poetry or short stories, or a series of essays that illuminate a wide variety of topics.

It's all about good writing, isn't it?

And it doesn't really matter where you do that writing.

I'm glad to call Colorado home, but I was glad to live in Kansas, too. Colorado gave me the inspiration for my first novel and I can now sit at my computer in my home office and watch the Gunnison River rise and fall with the seasons and see the surrounding mountains change from green to brown to white and back again to green and think how fortunate I am.

It isn't simply the river or the mountains that drive me to write, but they help. It isn't the history that surrounds me or the concern about the future of the arid West that provides the impetus to create, but that's part of it.

At the core, it's all about writing, story-telling, creating interesting characters, solving terrible dilemmas, describing the wet eyes and gut ache of emotion, reveling in the feeling of playing God for awhile and, in a prescribed period of time, creating a new world out of the confusing bits and pieces of the current one. I feel like I know Colorado well enough that I could write about it in Kansas or Wisconsin or New Jersey. I'd *rather* write about Colorado in Colorado but, in reality, it doesn't matter.

Let me tell you a widely known secret.

It's all about putting the right words together in the right order. Not everyone understands that or has the ability to carry it out.

Lots of people have a book in their head. Maybe half of them start to write it down. Maybe half of those get partway through. Maybe half of those keep pushing. Maybe a small one percent of those who are left actually get to The End. Many stop writing when they realize there is no roadmap to guide them to that last page. Many simply don't have the drive, the desire, the absolute hunger to get 'er done. E. L. Doctorow offers encouragement to those whose vision is limited: "Writing is like driving a car at night," he said. "You only see as far as your headlights go, but you can make the whole trip that way."

Still, most writers admit that it's grueling, hard work that is frustrating, agonizing, painful and often disappointing. But it's also thrilling and rewarding and joyous and uplifting.

So why do we do it? Why spend all that time and energy and deal with all that frustration and doubt and fear? Because there's something in us that drives us, that wakes us up in the middle of the night, that pesters us throughout the day. There's a voice in our ear that keeps coming up with ideas, phrases, plots that beg to be written down. Carlos Fuentes said, "One wants to tell a story, like Scheherazade, in order not to die. It's one of the oldest urges of mankind. It's a way of stalling death."

Finally, let me introduce you to a friend of mine. Richard Rhodes and I once shared an office while we worked in the advertising and sales promotion department of Hallmark Cards, Inc., in Kansas City, Missouri. An honors graduate of Yale University, Dick longed to write something other than straight-line corporate copy that helped to sell greeting cards. And, for that matter, so did I. Pretty soon we parted ways; I went into higher education and Dick went back east to write. He wrote a few novels that were well-received and then suddenly leapt into the lofty heights of the literary world by winning the Pulitzer Prize, the National Book Award and the National Book Critics Circle Award for *The Making of the Atomic Bomb*. He's since written other books including *Dark Sun: The Making of the Hydrogen Bomb*.

I tell you about him because he decided to write and found a way to do it. Despite the doubts and uncertainties of the profession he pondered now and again, he forged ahead. Rhodes said, "If you want to write, you can. Fear stops most people from writing, not lack of talent, whatever that is. Who am I? What right have I to speak? Who will listen to me, if I do? You're a human being, with a unique story to tell, and you have every right. If you speak with passion, many of us will listen. We need stories to live, all of us. We live by story. Yours enlarges the circle."

Thanks, Dick. I needed that.

So here's to you, writers who are interesting people, doing interesting things. And here's to all of you out there who are working to "enlarge the circle" and who "sit alone in a room and fight the language."

**Mara Purl** is the award-winning author of *The Milford-Haven* novels, which are based on her successful radio drama, *Milford-Haven, U.S.A.*, the first environmental radio soap opera and the only American soap opera ever licensed and broadcast by the BBC. Purl's screenwriting credits include *The Meridian Factor* and scripts for *Guiding Light*. She has had articles published by *Rolling Stone*, *Financial Times*, and an Associated Press assignment to cover the Apollo-Soyuz mission. An actress, Purl had a regular role on *Days of Our Lives*, and wrote and performed the one-woman play *Mary Shelley—In Her Own Words*.

Purl grew up in Tokyo, Japan, and received a performing and literary degree from Bennington College.

# Writing My Way from Effect to Cause: From Journalist to Journal-ist

## Mara Purl

THERE'S SOMETHING ABOUT being a writer that has us stand back. Back from life, that is, playing the role of the eternal observer. This was certainly the case when I was a journalist. My first professional job in the field of writing started at age fourteen, when I requested (actually, begged; no, insisted) that I be allowed to write a column for the *Mainichi Daily News*, the English-language version of a large metropolitan newspaper in Tokyo, where I grew up. The editor roared with laughter at my bravado, but I stood my ground. Still bemused, and tremendously tolerant, he eventually asked, "What do you want to write about?"

"I'd like to interview artists who visit Japan on tour." Though Mr. Shibata laughed again, I remained standing in front of his desk (and I did tower over him, even as a junior high schooler) until he relented.

"There's a press conference today," he offered. "Go there, then come back here and write it up."

"Yes, Sir!" I exclaimed, excitement tingling all the way to my toes. The press conference—some boring corporate announcement—was, for me, a thrill. I proudly returned to the newspaper office, inhaling the fragrance of newsprint, typewriter ribbon and eraser as though it were a rare elixir, infused for royalty. Mr. Shibata adjusted his glasses. All amusement left his expression as he pored over the words I'd carefully typed on a borrowed machine. I quivered with anticipation.

"This is good," he pronounced.

At last I could exhale.

"But this isn't journalism."

A sudden tightness constricted my chest. Seeing my evident panic, he sighed then suggested I pull up the extra chair near his desk.

"What you wrote is an essay. In journalism, we do it like this."

What followed was a lesson I remember to this day. It was more like a thesis tutorial than a mere teaching session. He spoke as a mentor to a mentee. He must have seen the lights going on in my eyes, because he rushed onward until he had revealed the Whole of Writing Wisdom as he knew it—and he knew journalism as the Buddha knows silence.

I flew back to the typewriter and fed a fresh piece of newsprint through the platen. I'd thought of a "lead"—something to start the story. Obeying this, and the other aspects of his instruction, I re-wrote the piece from top to bottom, knowing my prospective future as a columnist hung in the balance. Only if I successfully re-wrote the piece would Mr. Shibata consider me for his newspaper. Pulling the fresh story from the machine, I walked back to his office. He stopped clacking the keys of his own typewriter to read my edited piece. Looking up at me over the tops of his glasses, he said, "Good. When do you want to start?"

I was thrilled, honored, nervous, terrified, and—determined. I went on to write columns that still stand up to scrutiny. But looking back, I see an apparent contradiction I didn't notice at the time. By that point in my young life, I was also a budding artist in my own right. I'd started performing on television five years earlier; I was performing on stage before then. So what made me stand back from my own artistic endeavor to write about others?

I was responding to an irresistible urge to chronicle, observe, and record aspects of life that intrigued me. I would even go so far as to say that I needed to write about life as it was occurring for others in order to understand how it was occurring for me. This was my way of placing myself in context.

The ultimate experience of writing about something I would not be experiencing myself came when I covered the Apollo Soyuz mission. Since I wouldn't be hurtling through space myself, I did the next best thing: I got a special assignment to the Associated Press, and became the pool reporter in Mission Control. I was working with a group of seasoned pros I later named the "AP Space Kings." Between them, they'd covered every launch of the Mercury program, and every one of the Apollo missions to the moon.

As I hung on their every word, they shared stories, work methods, research tips, editorial styles and the sterling rules of journalist ethics. This code of ethics was put to the severest test during Apollo Soyuz when the astronauts had a problem that only the A.P. Space Kings could figure out. In deference to the astronauts, to their families, and to NASA, the Associated Press took the high ground and held the story. Here was a case where perhaps the most intriguing development of the mission was never told. Arguably, this wouldn't happen in today's climate of reportage. And some might say it shouldn't have happened then. "The public has a right to know," proclaims the old saw. That's a consideration for another essay.

My point here is that in journalism, we aim for impartiality. We make ourselves as invisible as possible, so our readers can see not only through us, but literally through us, our success thus being measured by the degree of our transparency. Yet, as I began to realize, even the cool, impartial lens of a camera can alter our view of life. It is, after all, an eye. And this is where I began to glimpse that the facts can, at times, obscure—rather than reveal—the underlying truth. In journalism this "lens factor" is seen as a liability. By the very nature of bringing attention, it magnifies, which is a form of distortion.

But what if, in the process, the lenses were to reveal things that could not otherwise be seen? If that were the case, my lens would become not a liability, but a major asset. I began to sense, no, intuit, that I might be on the planet not to overcome my own lens, but to share it. For me, the next chapter was writing non-fiction in longer forms. I wrote a few book-length corporate histories, fascinating chronicles of the building of personal empires.

I also co-wrote a nonfiction book about the acting business. *Act Right: A Manual for the On-Camera Actor* truly was a processing of both internal and external information. My dear friend Erin Gray and I wrote first-hand about the hundreds of foolish mistakes we made as we found our way through the hierarchy of television work. We also retroactively solved riddles of the entertainment business by interviewing colleagues from every department of the television and film business, creating a roadmap for young performers that had never existed before.

Good non-fiction offers not only a clear picture of what has transpired, but a reliable cipher to the code embedded in what for the reader is an unfamiliar world. The writer is driven to write something that has piqued his or her interest. For example, in *Time Present, Time Past*, Bill Bradley takes his readers behind closed doors in Washington D.C.; Jon Krakauer takes us to the summit of Everest in his riveting *Into Thin Air*; Katherine Shirek Doughtie puts us in the soccer mom's driver's seat of a woman trying to balance full-time work, full-time motherhood, and full-time dating in her *Aphrodite in Jeans: Adventure Tales about Men, Midlife and Motherhood*.

Each of these writers has not only keen observations, but astute theories they have developed to fit the facts they've observed. If this is the warp and woof of non-fiction writing, the facts might be described as the woof, the opinion as the warp. They are interwoven, creating a fabric unique to the moment, and to the voice of the observer. These writers don't necessarily claim objectivity. On the contrary, they offer their unique perspective. Still—they are stuck with what they've observed. To keep to their integrity, they cannot depart from those facts.

And yet this was a departure I began to crave. Freed from factual reportage, I could zoom my lens close-up on character flaws, life choices, bursts of unexpected dialogue, surprising connections between unlikely partners, and a host of other delicacies on life's menu, and serve them up in savory stews—or so I hoped. For all writers, life is stories. But it was time to tell the imaginative ones that kept bubbling up from the depths. Thus for me, the next chapter was fiction.

Mostly it was scripts at first. It was screenplays and teleplays that got optioned but never filmed. Eventually it was over one hundred for the BBC radio drama I created that reached 4.5 million listeners. I loved writing dialogue, which came as naturally as breathing. But rising like loaves in the corner of the kitchen was the narrative fiction that was to become the basic bread of my writing life.

If non-fiction writers are writing the text of life, what are we fiction writers up to? We're writing the subtext. And to do so, we need enough freedom from the facts—which live at the upper levels of the ocean—to dive deep beneath the surface. For here in the depths lurk the giant squids of conscience, passion, expectation, desire and destiny.

I attended a marketing seminar a couple of years ago during which a speaker said, "Fiction? No one cares! You made it up!" His comment was upsetting, sad, and revelatory. He was stuck with the mere text of life, missing the subtext. I wanted to ask him—what do we really have in life except our consciousness?

To paraphrase Ralph Waldo Emerson, we are, quite literally, what we think about all day. And how do we get at this internal dialogue? It seems to flit past us before we can notice. Various psychological techniques are employed to access this intriguing information. Jung's brilliant study of dreams might be our best shot at figuring out what and how we ourselves think subconsciously. But it's novelists who crack the code on the ongoing progression of waking thought, a process that might have begun with Jane Austen, or might even have begun with Lady Murasaki's Tale of Genji hundreds of years earlier.

In non-fiction we can't access what the people we're writing about can't even access for themselves. But in fiction we can reveal this extraordinary, and causative, layer of consciousness.

So what's the purpose of fiction? Truth-telling.

I started this essay with talking about writers standing back, being observers. To put this in personal terms, I could say that I started out at the effect of life. By that I mean, life was "out there," and what there was to do "in here" was notice, catalogue, reflect. I observed things happening to others, and thereby developed the habit of observing things happening to myself. My way of processing life issues was to write about them. My writing—with the hours, months and years it requires—gives me a great gift in return.

Through it I am literally writing my way out of my own stuck places.

To attempt to reveal something of my own internal thought process, it looks something like this: Did I fail at a crucial moment of my career? In fiction, I can revisit that disappointing conversation with my boss, the romantic breakup where I should have been brave, the audition where I should have been audacious. Are these mere indulgences of fantasy? I think they're more. I am revising the mortal history, reclaiming lost power, redeeming the pockets of selfishness, expunging the dark spots from my soul's x-rays.

Huge patterns have begun to emerge, designs I couldn't see at the outset of my saga as I was then too close to the threads. Now that some of the quilt's squares have been stitched into place, the larger pictures are beginning to emerge.

I'm a novelist now, engaged in the ongoing creation of a twelve-book saga of which only the fourth book has reached publication. The hours alone, the wrestlings with conscience, the tusslings with my editor, the exacting discipline rhetoric, these struggles tone my metaphysical muscles as though I'm training for the Olympics. None of my own flaws are exempt from scrutiny, be they pride or prejudice, resistance or laziness, ignorance or cowardice. In the face of tackling the creatures of the deep, there is simply no place to hide. In terms of the story telling, each character arc must have its own authenticity, with colors true enough, pathways parallel enough, to show up as rainbows through the reader's prism. And at this point in my journey, issues seem to vibrate in truest color through the eyes of one of my protagonist's personal diaries. Each of my novels ends with her long, rambling journal entries.

Readers tell me Samantha's journals are among their favorite parts of the books. Perhaps, then, I've written myself from journalist to journal-ist, in the process taking enough responsibility for my own life that I'm willing to admit my own thoughts cause much of what I'm experiencing.

**Dan Guenther** has a BA from Coe College and an MFA in English from the Writers' Workshop at the University of Iowa. Subsequent to leaving active duty in the Marine Corps, Guenther worked in Australia and was a high school principal for several years with the Bureau of Indian Affairs on the Choctaw reservation in Mississippi. He has worked as a training officer for the National Park Service, a consultant for Sun Microsystems, and taught at the Graduate School of Business, University of Colorado. His Vietnam trilogy, *China Wind* (Ivy, 1990) *Dodge City Blues* (Redburn Press, 2007), and *Townsend's Solitaire* (Redburn Press, 2008) is based on his combat experiences as a Marine officer in Vietnam. His fourth novel *Glossy Black Cockatoos* (Redburn Press, 2009) was the 2010 Colorado Authors League Award selection for Genre Fiction. He has also had poems published in small magazines and anthologies, most recently in the Australian journal, *Quadrant*, and in the anthology *Open Range: Poetry of the Reimagined West* (Ghost Road Press, 2007). His most recent book is a collection of poems titled *The Crooked Truth* (Redburn Press, 2010).

# Journey of Discovery

## Dan Guenther

MY WIFE AND I are having a late lunch at the Jumbo Thai on West Colfax in Denver, Colorado. Hidden among a seedy strip of old motels where the cross-country truckers like to hang out, Jumbo Thai is my kind of place—a hole in the wall, family-run operation, the kind of storefront restaurant that has sprung up all over America in the last thirty-five years as immigrants from Thailand, Vietnam, and many other countries have changed the nature of eating out in our country.

At 2:00 p.m. the heavy lunch rush is over, and we are the only customers. I finish my pad thai before my wife and, gazing about, pick up the August 31, 2007, *Rocky Mountain News* from the adjoining table. Reading leisurely, I notice that there is a front-page Spotlight feature on a writer I knew years ago at the University of Iowa. We were fellow students in the Writers Workshop program.

"Wow!" I said. "Denis Johnson has written a Vietnam novel. I'm amazed."

"Why does that amaze you? He's a great writer. What branch of the service was he in?"

"I don't think he was in the service. Of course, that really doesn't matter. But I would have never expected this."

Denis Johnson, the twenty-something poet I knew at the Iowa Writers' Workshop, looks good in the newspaper photo. He still has all his hair. Denis and I sat through a couple of workshops together in the early 1970s. Back then, there were a number of diverse soon-to-be-famous writers who were students at the same time: Tracy Kidder and Joe Haldeman; poets Rita Dove, Leslie Ullman, and Tess Gallagher, all of whom I knew, and T. Coraghessan Boyle, whom I didn't, to name just a few. Although I remember Denis mainly as a poet who published his first book at twenty, he was one of those rare people who were able to move freely between the poets and the fiction writers. His powerful short story collection full of sex, violence, and addiction, *Jesus' Son*, was published in 1992 and turned into a film in 1999.

Outside the workshop our paths would cross in the various Iowa City bars. There was The Mill, The Vine, Joe's Place where we all hung out until very late. I recall us both, deep in the depths of the Iowa winter, nodding to each other along the long bar at The Mill. This is the Denis I remember, fellow lover of the grain and the grape, as I was back then. But there were profound differences between us. Denis was a recently published young poet, a rising star in the workshop. I was a wild-eyed combat Marine back from nineteen months in Nam, someone in need of much help who didn't yet know enough to understand the depth of his need.

Tracy Kidder and Joe Haldeman were in Nam. I talked with both of them about their experiences. Joe eventually wrote *1968* and the classic science fiction war novel *The Forever War,* winner of Hugo and Nebula awards. Tracy, who went on to win the Pulitzer Prize and the National Book Award, eventually wrote his powerful memoir, *My Detachment*.

So, Denis writes a novel about Vietnam. But Denis wasn't there, or was he? I remember some things that Fred Exley, author of *A Fan's Notes* and my mentor at the University of Iowa Writers Workshop, said back in 1972 about his writing process. "I write not just to tell a story, that simple yearning to satisfy a creative urge, so-to-speak, I now write to discover the real story that is there, the story waiting to be told as the characters evolve." Fred told me this in a bar called Joe's Place, well into his cups. "And I write because I aspire to a more complete understanding of things, and writing has taken me to places where my understanding has become more complete as a result of my efforts," he added, swaying slightly and winking at my future wife. Fred had brought in William Styron to do a reading at the workshop. After the reading he, William Styron, and John Cheever were drinking hard.

My close relationship with Fred was much the same as that between Denis and his mentor, Ray Carver. I owe Fred Exley a lot for his interest and words of encouragement in the writing of my first novel, *China Wind*. He continued to coach me after we both left the workshop, back in the late 1970s, when my family lived in Mississippi. Fred would call me in the wee hours of the morning, often after having had a few drinks. Without him, I might not have written *China Wind*. I dedicated the novel to him.

Over the years, I find myself remembering the help and support Fred provided. It was also a time when I was beginning to come to terms with my own unreasoning fears, the aftershock of serving as a combat Marine in Vietnam, as a psychologist termed it. As Fred once pointed out to me, there would be no rewriting of that history; but maybe, in the process of writing fiction, I would gain a better understanding of that time. Perhaps I would even purge myself of the things that kept me awake at night. That notion played in my head over and over again, and as the writing moved forward, I found that I was returning to Vietnam to experience it in a different way. My writing was taking me to a place where my understanding was becoming more "complete," to use Fred Exley's word.

I think in the same way Denis Johnson has been to Nam without having ever gone. When I read his novel, *Tree of Smoke*, I experienced that deeper understanding that Fred had pushed for, and that vision all great writers are able to impart to their readers. Vision and understanding are the primary things I aspire to in my own writing.

It was during my time down in Mississippi that I began to ask myself why I kept writing. Over the years, in one form or another, I've continued to ask myself that question. I remember telling my oldest daughter, Ingrid, when she was about twelve, that I thought of myself as a storyteller. Ingrid is now thirty-two and I am trying to figure out this continued yearning to write both poetry and fiction. However, I have come to believe that the things within that move us toward writing either poetry or fiction are related, but different in their origins.

As a small boy, I had a wild imagination and I was always making up stories to entertain audiences ranging from adults to boyhood friends. That wild imagination grew into a yen for penning short stories. Eventually three of my books written for specific audiences were published. But the urge to express myself through poetry is much more complex, and arises out of a different yearning. The inspiration for my poetry usually comes from some impulse to gather together images that reflect my exploratory state of mind, and often lead me to some personal revelation. Later, I may refine what I have written, my personal definition of poetry being the art of using figurative and image-laden language that is often rhythmic, to teach and delight. Mostly I teach and delight myself.

When I write poetry, I am not concerned about a specific audience other than myself. What is important for me is to capture the emotional truth, so to speak, that is with me at that moment, my voice and choice of evocative images bringing the poem together, fused into a unified whole. The dynamic of my poetry writing is a very open-ended process, a free association of powerful images that align with my inward voice. Sometimes it works well, and other times the muse is clearly not with me.

In contrast, my fiction is more purposeful, and I am usually writing with what I am now calling my primary audience, my fellow veterans. I am much more conscious of craft. My fiction tends to be action-driven, and I feel an obligation to present characters that are precisely drawn and realistic, as opposed to presenting the surreal. They almost always face some problem or challenge that they must come to terms with. My characters also tend to reinvent themselves in the course of their development. At the end of the story they have changed, and come away having learned as a result of their experiences. Those characters have something to say and the stories I create reflect my own life.

Many years ago in Vietnam I met an Australian SAS captain who I much admired for his leadership style. He is the model for a major character in my novel, *Dodge City Blues*. After all these years, he lingers in my mind as a role model, someone who was a problem-solver and who inspired the confidence of those around him. I hope I do him justice in *Dodge City Blues*. In addition, given all the sad, stereotyped characterizations of both soldiers and Marines that we see in movies about Vietnam (i.e., *Platoon, Apocalypse Now*, etc.), I wanted to write a book that showed those who served conducting themselves honorably and in ways that demonstrated their problem-solving, team spirit, and ability to assume leadership roles when called upon.

*Dodge City Blues* was written in the early nineties, the sequel to my first novel, *China Wind*. However, for a number of complex reasons, including changing editors and changing book lists, it was never published and eventually returned to me. I learned a lot from that experience, and I'm glad I didn't compromise that book in response to certain editors pushing me to do things that ran counter to my artistic sense.

As a result of having my manuscript returned to me, I did a lot of soul searching, mapping out that huge fiction marketplace in my mind. It was clear to me that, given the various dimensions of fiction, I needed to sort out where I wanted to be in the marketplace. On one hand, I saw a great demand for the highly crafted genres of popular fiction in their various forms: mystery, romance, science fiction, and the thriller. As a member of the Rocky Mountain Fiction Writers, I knew people who were succeeding in the pursuit of writing what they called commercial fiction, stories written for pure entertainment. Nevada Barr, a writer and fellow National Park Service veteran whom I much admire, is someone I would hold up as an example of this kind of writing with her excellent mystery series set in the national parks.

On the other hand, I had friends and associates who aspired to write what they termed "serious fiction" in its various forms, collective mainstream as represented by the work of Philip Roth and John Updike; the more exclusive, literary fiction as we see in the work of Joyce Carol Oates and John Irving; and even truly visionary writing from the likes of Cormac McCarthy, Tony Morrison, and the great William Faulkner. I began to define my categories of serious fiction in greater detail. As a reader, the collective mainstream category was all about strong identification with the values presented in the author's works. My sophisticated marketing associates at Sun Microsystems called that kind of appeal "customer intimacy." The more exclusive, literary fiction category, as manifested by authors such as John Irving, a writer from whom I have learned a great deal, is all about achieving the superior in terms of artistic endeavor. Irving has bridged the literary and commercial; he is unique in having crossed all the borders of my humble fiction categories to create literary best sellers and win an Academy Award.

That was what the Iowa Writers Workshop was all about when I attended. Learning in that program had to do with developing individual expertise and excellence. I have writer friends who view that program as elitist, a kind of presumption of being the best. All I know is that the program helped me simply by way of being around other high-potential writing students, and authors like Irving. It was at the Iowa Writers Workshop that I first heard the term *visionary fiction*.

There are many great writers of visionary fiction. Today, I think of writers like Cormac McCarthy and Flannery O'Conner in that category, and maybe even Denis Johnson. The vision they bring to the reader may inspire and help relative to their pursuit of some higher purpose. I know that's what great teachers and leaders do, inspire by way of sharing their vision, where knowledge is often shared to further the rightness and future of that vision. *Jesus' Son* is a collection of short stories that would fall into my category of visionary fiction. *Tree of Smoke* would also fall into that category. Dow Mossman, my life-long friend from the workshop days, also wrote a visionary work. *The Stones of Summer*, is a coming of age novel comparable to J.D. Salinger's *Catcher in the Rye*.

Of course, I have a bias. Dow Mossman and I came of age together in the 1960s, during our college days. We ran away deep into Mexico for a time, wandering down through the Sonora Desert and across the Sierra Madres to Mazatlan. While I was in Vietnam, I wrote to Dow, and he included my letters in his book when it was published in 1972. When I submitted my application to the Iowa Writers Workshop, I included those published letters. I was later told those letters had caught the attention of Paul Engle, founding director of the Workshop, who remembered another captain of Marines by the name of Andre Dubus who once attended the workshop. Back when I applied, there weren't many Marine veterans interested in making application to the Iowa Writers Workshop.

I was fortunate to have a number of great teachers at the Iowa Workshop. I took a great Form of Poetry course with Donald Justice, who was a model for the behavior and values he expected in his students. Fred Exley, who was there only one semester, helped me recognize and seize some writing opportunities. But it was Norman Dubie who was especially helpful to me. Not only was he a writer whose work I would call visionary, but he was able to share his vision, and help energize his students to find their own vision. Those qualities set him apart from the other writing teachers I had there. Norman also helped me through some lingering health issues from Vietnam, issues that have weighed upon me all my life and still haunt me to this day.

As my process of mapping out the fiction marketplace moved forward, I began to understand how my writing needed to change, especially with the novel that had been remitted to me, *Dodge City Blues*. What was the vision I wanted to share? And what audience did I have in mind for such a book? In 1997 the answers to those two questions became clearer to me. First of all, I committed to my veteran audience. My writing then began to evolve to a new level, and I now truly understood that self-discovery process Fred Exley described. Call it a kind of fusion of internal, collective epiphanies where my real life experiences began to spill out on the page in fictional form. Some unique things were unfolding with respect to the emerging vision of *Dodge City Blues*. The way those unique things unfolded was, at times, even beautiful.

*Dodge City Blues* takes place in the Dai Loc and Dien Ban Districts of Quang Nam Province, in Vietnam. Back in 1969 some of us returned for a second time to Vietnam, and seeing no lasting results from our previous tours, encountered a sense of weariness and dissatisfaction, a kind of ennui a fellow Marine officer termed the "Dodge City Blues." The story picks up where *China Wind* leaves off, and then follows Sam Gatlin through his experience in Laos, continuing on into the bamboo hedgerows of the area the Marines knew as Dodge City. The narrative chronicles how Sam reinvents himself in order to respond to the changing demands placed upon him. His reinvention is the vision that drives the book. In 1998, I finally completed the rewrite of the book with that new vision as an anchor. However, shortly after I finished the rewrite, my computer crashed, and the file was lost. Due to competing work priorities, and increasingly complex health issues, I had to move on, hoping someday to recover that lost manuscript.

That *Dodge City Blues* manuscript remained limbo until 2006, when my daughter Ingrid's digital wizard husband Dave Scott was able to recover the file of that lost book from the old disabled hard drive. Dave recovered not only the original *Dodge City Blues* file, but also the lost file for my third book in the trilogy, *True Steel*, subsequently renamed *Townsend's Solitaire*. After that recovery, Redburn Press, already contracted to republish *China Wind*, offered to publish the other two books in the trilogy.

*Townsend's Solitaire* is the finale of my Vietnam trilogy, set in Yellowstone National Park in the 1980s. The novel explores Sam Gatlin's adjustments upon return to civilian life, and grew out of a yearning to make his story more complete. In 2005, that yearning was spurred on by an interesting set of circumstances.

Back in July 2005, I attended a reunion with the members of Mike Company, Third Battalion, Seventh Marines. I served with Mike Company on Operation Oklahoma Hills in May 1969. The Mike Company commander from that time, Paul Van Riper, retired as Marine Lieutenant General. At the reunion General Van Riper told me that as stories are retold by each of those who shared the experience, the narrative collapses, and as the heart of those stories is revealed through those collective perceptions, a truer knowledge unfolds of what happened and how things went down. The many Vietnam novels that have been published range widely in their subject areas with regard to what transpired. Drugs, race issues, leadership and teamwork: these meanings emerge in different ways. But at the heart of each piece of superior fiction about Vietnam are those core truths that enrich our understanding of that time and place. General Van Riper was saying some of the same things Fred Exley once said to me. When I returned to Colorado,

I felt I needed to revisit my old manuscript, *True Steel*, to finish my trilogy, and make whatever vision I had more complete. I set about editing *True Steel*, originally written in 1994, and renamed the book, *Townsend's Solitiare*.

Many of the Vietnam veterans I have talked to see things in Vietnam novels, including my own, from the perspective of their own unique story, meanings that I wasn't thinking of when I wrote. I am sure that is true of Denis's novel as well, as vets and others who read it. At the heart of *Tree of Smoke* are diverse ideas that describe how events happened, and make our understanding of its time and place more complete. The story shares a dark and enduring vision.

After he left the workshop, Denis went to live in New York to pursue a writing career that also involved teaching. My career took a different path. I left the U.S. to live in Australia for a couple of years and bounced around in a number of jobs. I was a high school principal on the Choctaw Indian Reservation in Neshoba County Mississippi, probably the hardest job I ever had. From Mississippi I left for Colorado, where I was a training officer for forty-two national parks in the Rocky Mountain Region, the most interesting job I ever had. After that, I ran the Rocky Flats Institute, training folks in the new technologies needed to clean up the environmental challenges at Rocky Flats Plant, the most important job I ever had. All the while I raised a beautiful family with my partner from Iowa before the advent of the Internet changed my life.

My partner encouraged me to get involved online with adult learning and the process of helping organizations manage for change, facilitating courses on leadership. During that period, I continued to reinvent myself, shedding some of the demons that had haunted me for years, and my career as a change agent took form. I worked for three large corporations, Rockwell International, EG&G, and Sun Microsystems, helping managers manage for change.

While I was with Rockwell, I was invited to teach the Leadership Enrichment Seminar to the senior cadets at the Air Force Academy. Much of that course content provided closure for some of the things that I was struggling with in *Dodge City Blues*. So I kept writing, and when my second daughter, Greta, and my son-in-law, Thomas, were serving their tours in Iraq, I found the inspiration that pushed me on to finish that lost manuscript. Once again I found myself processing those old demons, continuing on with that journey of discovery in which Fred Exley so firmly believed.

During that period, I know that Denis was also reinventing himself, as an educator, a poet, and a fiction writer. Like me, he was returning to Vietnam, seeing things from the perspectives of the characters in *Tree of Smoke*, each of them with their own unique story, stories in which Vietnam veterans will find unique meanings that Denis wasn't even thinking of when he created those characters.

Reflecting during that late afternoon lunch at the Jumbo Thai, it seemed to me that Nam unfolds in many books, each story unique, with some written by writers who may know that place only through their imaginations. Fred Exley, God rest his soul, was right. The process of writing is one of discovery, where the writer who aspires for a more complete understanding may find it, especially those truths of the human condition that unfold as the story is told. Fred Exley got to the Nam, in his own way, through helping me. And Denis Johnson went to Nam too while writing *Tree of Smoke*.

Those of us who served out on the broad rice plains of Dodge City or within the seething and soggy jungles along the Laotian border all have our own evolutions. Some of us find meaning for our Vietnam experiences over the years; others are just as sure that those efforts are futile. Many remain convinced that we were all complicit in what went down across that wine-dark China Sea. I believe that is one of the truths at the heart of *Tree of Smoke*, a truth waiting to be discovered by each one of us on our own terms. In the telling of stories a vision becomes enabled that inspires and endures in the memory of those who read the tale. And that, a tradition older than Homer and the hubris of Achilles, is as it should be, lest the service of those who were lost be forgotten.

Colorado author **Kathy Brandt** has published four mystery novels in her underwater investigation series (*Under Pressure, Dangerous Depths, Dark Water Dive, Swimming with the Dead*) featuring SCUBA diver and underwater crime scene investigator Hannah Simpson. Brandt has just completed her fifth book; a mainstream novel titled *Out of Sight* and is at work on a memoir with her son. Brandt taught writing at the University of Colorado for ten years before deciding to write full time. Her articles have appeared in *Cruising World, Sailing, Yachting, Women's Sports and Fitness,* and scores of other publications.

# What the Hell Am I Doing?

### Kathy Brandt

AT LEAST ONCE a day I ask myself why I spend half my waking hours writing. The time between the first page and the last, between the concept and the completion, is a labyrinth of Escher stairs. I avoid placing my fingers on the computer keys each morning until I have no choice, until I have extinguished all excuses. I am confused, fearful, and impatient. I don't know what to write. I can't think of the right metaphor or description. It's hard, it's stressful, and it's all consuming. I feel incompetent. I am unsure. I am a crappy writer trying to find a minute of excellence.

Many writers tell me they write for the pure pleasure of writing. I envy them and wonder where I've gone wrong. Why can't I be like them? Instead I sit at the computer, blank screen yelling at me to write something, anything. I check my email. I Google CNN. I wander the house, looking for distraction and feeling guilty. I spend entire days sitting in my office not writing.

I invoke the muses—Calliope, Euterpe, Thalia, Clio. I'll take anyone. None accept my invitation. No words set my mind on fire or spill tears onto my keyboard. I wallow in my empty mind. If you think that I sound tormented, you are right. If you wonder why any rational person would engage in such self-inflicted suffering, know that I wonder the same.

Yet I write. Some reasons are easily defined. I write for the experiences that ultimately paint my writing—perusing third world markets made vibrant by mangoes and island patois; visiting jails saturated by iron bars, a man's blank stare, a guard's indifference; tracking dark green disks, turtles that glide through turquoise; sitting beside a cop as frantic parents demand he find their fourteen-year-old daughter; finding Tony Blair, his sailboat anchored beside ours in a Mayreau harbor.

And I write to be published. I write because there are things I need to say and because I want people to hear them. I want my readers to see the ocean's sponges, the magic of a manta ray as it flies through salt water. I want them to know what is at stake in our oceans—what we have to lose. I want them to feel what it means to suffer from manic depression, to pace the floors in a prison cell, to stand on a bunk with a noose around one's neck. To understand that sometimes we fail others.

But the real reason I write? I simply have no choice. Something in my chest, my stomach, my gut, demands that I write. It goes well beyond the need to eat or sleep. Perhaps it is the compulsion to make something, like the carpenter crafts a chair, the sculptor molds a figure, the seamstress sews a gown. It's the need to make right sentences, find the perfect cadence of words.

When I'm not writing I am like a chained terrier, unable to nip at the tires of a passing car. So I have to write. As a result my life is unbalanced. I write to the exclusion of most other daily activities. Which means when I finish a piece, I ramble around the house trying to fill the void. Sometimes I clean. I take time to have lunch with friends. I pick up weights—do a dozen bicep curls, a sit-up or two. But what I'm really doing is not writing. I'm having lunch and not writing. I'm cleaning and not writing. In my chest is the writing, in my head the next project.

I'm sure much of my compulsion is related to my upbringing—the Roman Catholic guilt and the pot-roast-and-peas work ethic. Forty-two years since I've been to Mass and I can still hear the cadence, the indecipherable songs of mystery and ceremony. *Sanctus, Sanctus, Sanctus, Dominus Deus Sabaoth. Pleni sunt coeli et terra gloria tua. Hosanna in excelsis. Benedictus qui venit in nomine Domini. Hosanna in excelsis.* I know the "thou shalt nots," the proceedings of confession, penance, and forgiveness. I knew what was expected by the time I was five years old.

My Midwestern upbringing had none of the allure of such writers as Eudora Welty. From the age of two she understood that every room in her home existed for reading. She describes bookcases laden with Dickens, Twain, Stevenson, Wharton and Mann. We had one bookshelf in our house. It contained a dictionary, a couple of bound issues of Reader's Digest, and a set of encyclopedias that my mother bought from a door-to-door salesman.

I treasured a book of children's rhyme that resided in our bedroom, a volume illustrated in bold strokes of primary colors. One day, my infant sister set about dismembering it during her afternoon nap. She tore at words and chewed on each shredded rhyme, then ripped and shredded another. She ate those stories, transforming the beautiful blue bound book into jagged pages of interrupted prose and pictures. I wrapped the remains in tissue, and hid them in my closet.

My mother rarely had the time to read—five kids, she spent her days draping wet sheets on clotheslines, sweating in the steam of her iron, or searching the grocery shelves for the cheapest can of creamed corn. My father was at his dairy at dawn to meet the farmers who brought fresh milk and eggs. He whistled to Nat King Cole, swung my mother into his arms, fingers snapping to the rhythm, and was a master of the joke. Whatever I learned about the perfectly timed finish, I learned from his punch lines.

I made my own way to the library. Sitting on the floor in the children's section where books were conveniently located on a single bottom shelf, I made my way across that shelf from A to Z, then began again.

I was enthralled by words. I knew someday I would scrawl my own across a page. Later, I did. As a teenager in the grip of hormones, I penned vignettes and hid them in a notebook under my bed. It took me a long time to "come out," some forty years in fact. It began with one article, and then another until dozens had been published in one magazine or another.

When I began writing my novel, I did it just to see if I could. I didn't have a shelf full of books with titles like *How to Write a Best Seller* in my library. I'd never taken a class explaining the techniques of a well-structured book, developed characters, or vibrant settings. Was it even remotely possible that I could simply tell a story in three hundred pages? There's a lot to be said for learning by doing.

No one was more surprised than I when that book was published, followed by three more. I passed snowy days transported to the tropical places that I wrote about in those books. It was almost easy to write then about hibiscus-scented breezes and the taste of coconut milk when the temperature outside was minus ten.

Now the good days keep me going, the days I peck out a word that turns to a sentence that turns to a page, the times my characters take on lives of their own and decide events for me, the times my fingers fly across the keys. Hours go by and I forget lunch. Sometimes I have an appointment. Just fifteen more minutes, I tell myself and end up late.

I admit that I am driven. I protect my time and space. I conduct my day like a nine-to-five job. This can be difficult. How do you convince a friend, who is sure all you're doing is watching soaps and picking up a pen for a few minutes each day, that no you really can't meet her for coffee? How do you tell her that the boss—that's me—will be angry at…well, me?

So I hide out. I live on seven acres down a long gravel driveway in the Colorado mountains. Only the invited make their way to my door and only when the road is clear. Even UPS will not venture up the hill in the snowy season. And the snowy season at 8,800 feet is every day for months on a northern exposure.

I've got a system. When I'm creating a story on cold winter mornings, I'm up just long enough to make coffee. Then I head back to my bed, nestle under the down comforter, and perch my laptop on my knees. By noon, I've got a fire in the wood burner and I've found the sun in the bay window. In the summer I throw off the comforter and take my laptop outside to the deck where hummingbirds buzz the feeder.

When I have a story with a beginning, middle, and an end, I go to my office, a tiny room with two glass filled walls. I go there for the desk—a place to spread out, shelves where my research is piled, a place to perch my storyboard, a place to rewrite. I love the light, but sometimes I am too intent to notice what's occurring on the other side of the glass. Sometimes I look up, surprised to see a mule deer or an elk pulling leaves off an aspen. But mostly I'm unaware, too busy moving scenes, dropping characters, cutting, pasting, adding, subtracting, and toying with prose. Yesterday, three black bears ambled around the corner of our house. Siblings, I think. They wrestled outside my window as I wrote of razor wire prison walls. I put them in my story.

And then one day, I'm startled to find I've finished. I don't know how I got off of those twisted stairs. I just did.

**Mario Acevedo** was born in El Paso, Texas. He has lived all over the United States and paid his bills working as a military helicopter pilot, paratrooper, engineer, art teacher to incarcerated felons, software programmer, and various other jobs that involve watching a clock. He managed to escape the cubicle when he was selected as an artist-in-residence for Arte America in Fresno, California. Later, he was deployed overseas as a soldier-artist for the U.S. Army in Desert Storm. During all this time, Mario kept busy writing novels. After years of collecting rejection slips, he finally got published and tumbled into the world of vampire detectives, alien gangsters, zombies, nymphomaniacs, and werewolves. Mario lives and writes in Denver, where he collects weird but true stories that prove life always trumps art.

# Cowboy Up!

## Mario Acevedo

WHEN THE WORLD gives you more than your share of misfortune and you falter, remember the wisdom of this bumper sticker:

> *Are you going to cowboy up*
> *or are you going to lie there and bleed?*

As a writer, I've had plenty of setbacks and have had to learn to cowboy up, something you'd expect from a writer who lives in the West. However I don't see myself as a western writer even though I've lived most of my life out west, wandering through Texas, New Mexico, California, and have now set roots in Colorado.

Why don't I see myself as a Western writer? Because I keep getting stuck on clichés. I'm talking about a Western writer with a capital W as in Western. The Marlboro man. *Hombre*! Big cowboy hat. Cowboy boots. Yoked shirts, tight jeans, and a fancy silver buckle. A gimped walk from being thrown off rodeo bulls. Stories of hunting, riding the range on roan ponies, and saving the day with a trusty Winchester .30-.30.

Me? I don't even own a cowboy hat. I do have a pair of cowboy boots but it took me a while to get used to them. When I first wore them, I felt I was clomping around in dude-ranch drag. No fancy silver buckles for me. When I gimp, it's because my leg fell asleep.

If there's one attribute common to a real cowboy and a successful writer, it's that each must persevere. In the struggle to get published, one can expect apathy, skepticism, lots of rejection, and occasionally, outright scorn.

As a writer I've persevered. In order to get published, I had to cowboy up. So if I'm not a Western writer, what kind of a writer am I?

I hope I'm a good one. If we're looking for labels, then let's go down the list.

Why don't we begin with my ethnic heritage, a convenient if lazy way to identify a writer. Call me Latino, Hispanic, or Chicano. One of them brown-skinned literary types.

On the other hand, I'm not so literary because I write vampire novels. My series' hero is Chicano because we have lots of Chicanos as criminals, lawyers, criminals, cops, doctors, more criminals, but none as a vampire-detective. I feel that with my contribution the canon of American literature is a little more encompassing.

My protagonist's heritage is a reflection of my upbringing. Write what you know. I know I like frijoles and tortillas. As for my heritage, had I been born in Duluth, Minnesota, of Norwegian Lutheran stock, my vampire could've been mistaken for Garrison Keillor. Think *Lake Wobegone of the Undead*.

Why do I write about vampires? The flip answer is that vampires found me, but that's not what happened. As a young man, I didn't like to read fantasy and certainly not anything about vampires. My exposure to the world of undead bloodsuckers was limited to cheesy movies on late-night cable TV.

My turn toward fantasy started after I read Charlaine Harris' *Dead Until Dark*, about a mind-reading waitress and her vampire boyfriend. I enjoyed Harris' humorous and compelling take on humans interacting with supernatural creatures. Her book gave me license to venture into the fantasy world and remake it as my own.

I also consider myself a mystery writer. I like the structure of a who-done-it. In a mystery novel you're forced to grapple with the story question and the competing agendas of the characters. Give it to me gritty and served up dirty and graphic.

Okay, I'm a fantasy-mystery writer. Let's turn to a more basic question. Why did I become a writer in the first place?

I blame my sixth-grade English teacher, Ms. Anderson. She paired up the students in her class and gave us until the middle of the semester to write a book.

At that time, a young and slender William Shatner was on the original Star Trek on TV. My writing partner and I loved that show and we decided to write our own space saga. We drafted plot ideas, designed the ship and the crew's uniforms (nifty-looking rank insignia was extremely important), and sketched maps of the galaxy.

Six weeks passed and it was time to submit our assignments. The other students' work included stories about the adventures of a lost dog, or how Santa's sleigh was wrecked and that he delivered presents on skis. The hand-illustrated books were stapled to the classroom bulletin board.

My writing partner and I had no book.

Ms. Williams was surprised because we were good students and knew we hadn't shrugged off the assignment. We told her we didn't finish our book and showed her a three-inch binder full of notes, drawings, and maps. The story had simply grown too big. Ms. Anderson was impressed enough with our efforts that she gave us an A.

What that assignment started was a running narrative in my head. I couldn't go anywhere without weaving my surroundings into a story. Most of the time I was lost in a daydream. I'd go grocery shopping and my characters were raiding enemy supplies for provisions. A drive across town was a run through a blockade of marauding intergalactic buccaneers.

My story evolved from the Star Trek scenario to that of an Earthman marooned on a planet beset by civil war, pirates, and aerial combat between giant flying machines. Edgar Rice Burroughs' books about John Carter of Mars were a big influence. I was going through puberty and I spent many moments alone imagining what kind of exotic body could belong to a Martian woman with a name like Llana of Gathol. With my imagination stoked by Burroughs and Star Trek, I created my own world and filled sketchbooks with maps, drawings, and narratives.

There's an unwritten rule that you should keep such obsessions private, especially if you live in a small town. I learned that lesson after I befriended the son of preacher of my church and in a moment of comradeship, shared my drawings and maps. Afterwards, he gossiped to the kids in Sunday school that I was a loony living in cuckoo land. So, thereafter, I kept the stories to myself.

In college I had to get serious about life, unfortunately. The stories were crowded from my head by my engineering studies. After graduating, I was sucked into another fantasy world that didn't allow much opportunity for daydreaming: the United States Army.

Seven years later I was a civilian again. I had plenty of time to daydream and the narrative returned. I fueled my musings with books and after slogging through a particularly boring tome, I got hooked with the most dangerous thought in the world: "I can write better than this!"

I bought a Tandy computer from Radio Shack and sat down to write my first novel, a post-apocalyptic thriller. A hundred pages later, I was stuck in a corner, trapped by the most basic of story questions. What was the story about? What was at stake? Why should anyone care to read this?

So I plunged into another manuscript. Then another. And another. I persevered. I studied plotting and dialog. I became confident enough in my stories that I began to send out query letters. And I collected a thick file of rejections. Still, I persevered.

It wasn't until I moved to Denver that my writing process changed for the better. I joined the Rocky Mountain Fiction Writers, a nonprofit organization dedicated to writers of novel-length commercial fiction, meaning: no poems, no short stories, no screenplays, no meandering navel-gazing literary works. They wanted genre: romance, mystery, thriller, or fantasy. A story with a plot you could chew.

This was the first time I'd been around published writers. In retrospect, it was an obvious place for an aspiring writer to start. Learn from those successful in the business. Up until then, my writing experience had been to slave away at the keyboard and learn what I could from books and magazines. I understood a little of the craft but I needed to learn more. However, the one creative writing class I took was a disaster. Our instructor had issues, such as not knowing how to act like a human being. The experience was like having a dog bite my leg. I cowboyed up and moved on.

Rocky Mountain Fiction Writers was a refreshing change of attitude and culture.

No snarling dogs.

No pussy cats either. They were and are demanding. Ernest Hemingway said that every writer needs a built-in, shockproof shit detector. My fellow writers in RMFW were eager to use my manuscripts to calibrate their shit detectors.

Despite the guidance and encouragement, my growth as a writer took years. I cranked out two more manuscripts before my critique group said I'd found my voice, as that of a smart ass.

I like how satire illuminates the absurdities of life. What better way to puncture a windbag than by knifing him with sarcasm? How many times have we been tripped up by the ironies of our making? When that happens, the best way to cope is with a laugh.

In one of my draft novels, I play with that satire when I show two space pirates about to be executed.

One says, "Sons of bitches. First they feed us. Then they hang us."

The second answers, "Look at the bright side. At least we won't die hungry."

For all my attempts at hard-boiled action and black humor, manuscript number six disappeared down a hole of indifference from all the agents I queried. I didn't even get back so much as a form rejection letter.

So, would I lie there and bleed or would I cowboy up?

Thanks to the influence of *Dead Until Dark*, I then decided to write about the most ridiculous premise I could think of: a vampire detective investigates an outbreak of nymphomania at the Rocky Flats Nuclear Weapons Plant near Denver. And miraculously, this story got the attention of a literary agent. I had heard him speak at a writers' conference and when he mentioned that he'd sold a zombie novel, I thought, zombies are smelly creatures with few social graces. How can they compare to vampires?

I followed this agent from the workshop and gave him my elevator pitch—in a hotel elevator. He offered his card and after a series of emails, agreed to represent me.

My agent told me that in this genre, he could sell a series easier than he could sell a stand-alone. Did I have more stories?

"But of course," I answered. "I'm drafting the sequel as we speak." I put the phone down and started writing book number two.

While my agent was priming his contacts in the publishing world, I had this nagging reminder in my head. I used to work at Rocky Flats and recalled this note of caution from a security briefing: *Since you work at Rocky Flats, if you ever write anything about Rocky Flats, you must submit the material to the Department of Energy for a declassification review.*

I hadn't worked at the Flats for years, and surely, I wouldn't have to submit my story about vampires, nymphomaniacs, and extraterrestrials to the government?

I contacted the Department of Energy's Document Control in Germantown, Pennsylvania, and explained the situation.

"It's a formality," the clerk on the other end of the phone assured me. "It'll take two weeks, tops."

"Two weeks?" my agent asked after I'd told him. "It'll be more like two months. I'm used to dealing with foot-dragging bureaucrats."

Two weeks passed by. Then four weeks. Nothing.

I called Document Control. They said the review of my manuscript kept getting sidelined by more pressing assignments.

After two months, I called again.

Document Control asked, "What manuscript?"

"A-ha," I replied. I had the foresight to send the manuscript Delivery Confirmation and I gave the clerk the date and time the delivery had been made to his office.

"Hold on a second," he said. "It's right here. Your manuscript has been reviewed and released as unclassified."

This process delayed the publication of my book by several months. My agent and I decided that when life gives you lemons, it's for the lemon twist in a martini. We'd use that declassification review to our advantage. He pitched my manuscript as the first and only vampire story to be declassified by the Federal Government. Your tax dollars at work.

In retrospect, as a marketing gimmick, I should've put classified information in the story. That way the final copy would've been redacted with big black marks and the reader would be left wondering what our government did not want us to know about vampires.

Given the government's record of lies and obfuscation in its nuclear weapons program, I had little problem weaving together a story from the black cloth of official history and denials. All perfect grist for my work of social satire disguised as a fantasy-mystery novel, *The Nymphos of Rocky Flats*.

Getting this book published only took six manuscripts and seventeen years. I had to cowboy up many, many times.

Every writer goes through a similar, if maybe shorter, ordeal. I became aware of this when I was going over the copy edits for my second novel, *X-Rated Bloodsuckers*. At the time I had just finished reading *The Great Gatsby*. The publisher's afterword included the editor's revision letter Maxwell Perkins had sent to F. Scott Fitzgerald. In the letter, Perkins pointed out "a certain slight sagging in chapters six and seven," and went on to offer other points of criticism.

Incredibly, such comments reminded me of those my editor had sent to me. Literary genius did not come easy to F. Scott Fitzgerald even if he wrote about rich guys on Long Island instead of horny vampires.

I felt such a kinship with Fitzgerald, though had we ever met (using a time-portal fantasy thingy), he would have probably asked me to park his car.

Like Fitzgerald, if you want to succeed as a writer, you must continue to persevere. After hard work and luck, you'll finally get published. Specifically, you will get "the call." An editor will offer to publish your book.

The presumptive notion is that you'll get showered with money and glory. Your life as a mortal human will have stopped. You are now one of the anointed few. Your words will be cataloged in libraries and live forever. The most physical labor you're now required to do is lift a pen to autograph your books, or endorse checks, and to sip your daily lunchtime cocktail.

The reality is this: Don't quit your day job. Unless magical stardust falls on you—and it has for some people—expect to have two jobs, one writing and the other that keeps you off street corners. No matter what happens, if you're serious about writing, be ready to cowboy up.

Once you get published, regardless of how much money you get or don't get, the bar is raised. People—your agent, your editor, fellow writers and readers—expect more. More of everything. More stories, better and richer than before. More promotional copy. And most importantly, more sales.

Once you do get published, celebrate your success and organize a book launch party. You'll be overwhelmed by the turnout. Relatives, work colleagues, and random acquaintances will show up. Get ready to hear:

"I didn't know you could write."

"*You* wrote a book?"

"Who's going to star in the movie adaptation?"

After fielding the questions, you'll get hand cramps from signing so many of your books. It's a rush. But I warn you, few book signings will ever be as rewarding.

For example, shortly after my first book came out, I got a call from a district marketing manager for Borders Books. She wanted to know if I was interested in signings at their Arizona and California stores. I said yes but wondered what they knew that I didn't. Was there a groundswell of fans in the southwestern United States?

After a lot of corporate huffing and puffing, I was scheduled for a signing at the Phoenix Biltmore Borders. Posters with my book cover flanked the entrance and announced: Author Mario Acevedo signs tonight.

The store manager took me upstairs to a table stacked with my books and decorated with more posters. A dozen chairs were arranged in front of the table and amazingly, half of the chairs were occupied.

I was touched that six complete strangers had come out to see me. I had heard enough demoralizing store appearance anecdotes from other authors to appreciate this modest but welcome audience.

I started to introduce myself and thank the people for attending.

They replied in a chorus, "We're not here for you. We're waiting for the French club."

En masse, they scurried to the nearby café, where they sat with their backs to me. They peeked over their shoulders—striving to avoid eye contact—and scoped out the floor to see if I was still there.

The manager returned and wondered where everyone had gone. I pointed to the café.

He surveyed the empty chairs and the stacks of my books. The manager sighed with annoyance at all the trouble he had gone through for nothing and said to me, "I thought you were famous."

Apparently not.

We writers fantasize ourselves as another Truman Capote or David Sedaris filling auditoriums jammed with fans who've paid to see us and hear us read. Hundreds will hold their breaths as they wait for our jeweled insights and observations.

Again, reality crashed into me like a dump truck. (You see why I like satire. Most of the events in my life prove that God does indeed have a sense of humor.) At my debut book launch signing, I read what I thought was a killer scene. My selection was to be a roller coaster ride through the gamut of human experience. Writing fiction is all about emotional manipulation and I'd show this crowd that I was the master manipulator.

What I planned were peals of laughter and startled gasps of astonishment. If I were lucky, tears. Instead, my jokes sputtered and died like damp matches. My telling, poignant vignettes made eyes cloud over with a dull grayness. People checked their watches and became suddenly fascinated with the lint on their sleeves. And these were my friends. Everyone else slumped in their chairs like homeless vagrants buzzed on Night Train.

I ended my reading with a thunderbolt of a joke. Or so I thought.

After the punch line, the response was a roomful of sleepy faces, blinking like a den of bears awakening from hibernation. They took in the silence and stared at me, taking a moment to realize that I had stopped talking. They began a slow mechanical clap, both out of ingrained politeness and to return the circulation to their arms.

Even if this happens to you, I hope you'll keep writing and before too long, your second book will be ready. Don't be surprised if the invitations to your new signings are met with guarded hesitation.

"Another book?"

"I haven't even read the first one."

"How many books are you going to write?"

"Don't you have a day job?"

During my time of literary apprenticeship I used to hear how much effort an author had to devote to promoting his or her books. Now as an author I'm expected to have a website, a blog, a newsletter, a MySpace page, be on FaceBook, finagle radio, television, and magazine interviews; in general, be everywhere, all the time.

You'll attend writing and fan conferences, which are fun. Now for the God-having-a-sense-of-humor part: During one of the author autograph sessions, you will at one time find yourself sitting next to the headliner, a *New York Times* bestselling author. However gracious this person may be, the experience will be an exercise in literary masochism. You'll be forgotten behind a scattering of your books while the conference staff carts in boxes of the headliner's novels. The mob of fans will assume you are an assistant. If you're lucky, you might get a few sympathy sales.

Still, you persevere. You keep writing and reading. You study the competition, your eyes sharper now to the details that separate great from merely good. You learn not to complain about the apparent unfairness of the publishing business. Like when an unknown writer gets an advance big enough to buy your town. This writer's work is lauded as the new Great American Novel and wins so many awards that his or her mantle collapses under the weight of them all. Hollywood stampedes for the movie rights.

Meanwhile, your books bob up on various lists. Little by little, the breaks come your way.

You'll get email from fans. People will ask you to guest blog. You'll be introduced at parties, not by your day job persona, but as a writer. You'll go to a signing in a distant city where you're sure no one has a clue who you are and astonishingly, there'll be readers waiting for your autograph.

Fans. Waiting to meet you. *The author.*

If this is what you want, and I hope you do, what advice can I share to minimize the number of times you have to cowboy up?

How about this primer on author-reader etiquette?

Remember that writers, the good ones anyway, are anxiety-ridden wretches. These writers worry themselves to a state of apoplexy about their work. Don't mistake their withdrawn manner for arrogant aloofness. Writers spend hours and hours, days and days, hunched over a keyboard, trying to make sense of the babble in their heads. When they go out in public, authors are like moles that have broken through the lawn. They squint at the light and are not sure if what approaches is another mole (hopefully eager to buy drinks) or a fox about to devour them. Treat authors like the dirty but friendly varmints that they are.

Which leads to this quote by Lawrence Kasdan: "Being a writer is like having homework for the rest of your life."

Every writer has enough to read for three lifetimes. A writer's desk looks like a paper factory that got hit by a barrage of tornadoes and a dozen earthquakes.

Here's my first no-no. For God's sake, do not show up at a signing with your manuscript in hand and expect the author to fall over himself in his eagerness to read it. Even if the author really likes you, I mean has the major let's-go-to-your-hotel-room-now-and-pretend-that-you're-not-married hots for you, what he sees is another mountain of words to plow through and he's already a week behind on his most pressing deadline.

Trust me, suppose he takes the manuscript and you wind up trading diphthongs under the covers, he may be conjugating your verbs but what's running through his mind is how to resolve his novel's pesky subplots and when will he receive his next royalty check.

Likewise, don't give an author a signed copy of your book unless asked for. Make nice chit-chat, say a couple of flattering remarks about the author's latest novel (you can never get too good at faking sincerity), and don't be surprised if the author asks for your book, or even better, sends an email that he bought a copy and enjoyed it.

Second big no-no: Don't say to an author that you've got a great idea for a book but since you're not a writer, you'll be happy to dictate the story and split the profits. Again, writers have more work than days on this earth, so expect a quick "No thank you."

If the story is that important to you, you'll learn how to write it. But don't be surprised that as you're writing the story, you learn that maybe it wasn't such a good idea after all. In that case, go on to your next idea. Just don't give up.

The final big no-no: When you meet a writer, don't explain what was wrong with her work. If the writer agrees, she already knows. If she doesn't agree, she's heard enough from a plague of scurvy reviewers. And what's the author to do, rewrite the book?

No matter what kind of a writer you are: western, fantasy, romance, mystery, or where you are in the writing process, you'll always have challenges. Embrace your triumphs, however fleeting they may seem at the time, and learn from your setbacks. Set your sights high.

Persevere.

Always cowboy up.

**Susan Tweit** is plant ecologist who began her career studying the life and times of sagebrush, what grizzly bears eat, and wildfire behavior. She turned to writing when she realized that she loved the stories behind the data more than collecting the data itself. Her writing on "the community of the land—nature and the places we live—" has won regional and national awards, a ForeWord Book of the Year Award, the Colorado Book Award, the Colorado Author's League Top Hand Award, and an EDDIE in the magazine world. Her twelve books include *Walking Nature Home: A Life's Journey*, available in print, on Kindle, and soon in audiobook form, and *Colorado Scenic Byways: Taking the Other Road*, chosen by Colorado's former governor Bill Ritter as his personal gift to dignitaries visiting the state, including Hillary and Bill Clinton, and Michelle and Barack Obama. Her work appears in magazines and newspapers, ranging from *Audubon* to *young*ARTS, and the *Los Angeles Times* to *Popular Mechanics*, and is heard on community radio station KHEN FM. She lives with her husband, sculptor Richard Cabe, on a formerly decaying industrial site in the heart of Salida.

# Writing My Way Home

## Susan Tweit

THE ROOM WHERE I write is small, not much bigger than a walk-in closet, really. But size, in this case, does not matter, because my writing space opens to the outside via a rectangular bay of windows just above desk height with a view encompassing a fair portion of the landscape I call home. Each morning before I begin writing, I scan that view the way a farmer habitually checks the sky to see what the day will bring. Through the pane to my left, my eyes trace the undulating skyline just across the Arkansas River, where the morning sun rises over piñon-pine and juniper-dotted ridges that locals call the Arkansas "Hills" (their tallest points rise to only around ten thousand feet elevation, far lower than the numerous Fourteeners, peaks higher than fourteen thousand feet that form the skyline on the west side of the valley).

I follow that ridgeline to the right with my gaze until it descends into the gap of Bighorn Sheep Canyon where the Arkansas River cuts out of the mountains bound for the Great Plains and its eventual rendezvous with the Mississippi some 1,400 miles away. Past the canyon and now looking straight ahead, my eye climbs a sinuous dark-forested ridge to the rocky wall of the Sangre de Cristo Range, its peaks spaced as closely as the studs on a pit-bull's collar. The rhythmic alternation of peak-saddle-peak draws my gaze to the right, following the range as it marches west until it dips to 9,012-foot-elevation Poncha Pass, where it merges with the main spine of the Rockies.

Moving farther west, my eyes swoop up to the peaks on the Continental Divide, marked by the broadly pyramidal summit of Mount Ouray, named for a Ute leader whose people still frequented this valley less than a century ago. Ouray's shoulder-like ridges muscle higher than the peaks around it, raising its pointed summit to almost seven thousand feet higher than where I sit. If I tilt my chair forward and crane my head to the right, looking through the west window of the bay that my desk is built into, my gaze traces the Continental Divide north, beginning with the snow-splotched summits of Chipeta and Pahlone, named for Ouray's wife and son.

Below that lofty skyline, my view takes in the decidedly domestic middle-ground of my small town, with its ornately decorated brick downtown blocks, spreading shade trees, and front porch-bedecked houses dating to the twin mining and railroad booms of the late 1800s. In our formerly industrial wrong-side-of-the-tracks neighborhood, trains once thundered by on the mainline railroad tracks across Ditch Creek, shaking our block with their passage. The concrete walking/biking path that replaced the tracks a decade ago now carries a steady parade of cyclists, some pulling kids in weather-tight trailers; plus baggy-panted teens on skateboards, joggers, and walkers of all ages, many escorted by canine companions.

In the immediate foreground, my view takes in a relic of our property's industrial heritage, the rusted roof of the corrugated tin shed that once held pumps and valves controlling the flow of oil from tanker cars parked on a siding just across Ditch Creek to storage tanks where our house now sits. Just below my bay of windows stretch the linear raised beds of our kitchen garden, nested inside the concrete wall built to contain spills from those aboveground tanks. The wall and its seating-height raised beds now contain a riot of organically-grown tomatoes, basil, sugar-snap peas, carrots, and lettuce mixes; spinach, broccoli, beets, summer squash, cilantro, strawberries, and feathery asparagus. Lapping up to the kitchen garden is a wildflower-studded "lawn," a restored native plant community that my husband, Richard, and I have carefully nurtured to re-green this formerly decaying industrial property, including curly-leaved blue grama grass and feathery needle-and-thread, along with desert Indian paintbrush, Rocky Mountain penstemon, and gold blanketflower.

Visitors often ask how I can write with such a gloriously distracting view, and I say I couldn't write as well without this view. The peaks, the patches of grassy, bald and green-velvet aspen groves on hazy mountainsides, the pointillist pattern of stunted piñon pines covering the hills across the river, the nearby roofs and traffic, and my own patch of restored wildness with its scent of sagebrush and sun-dried soil remind me of why I spend my days wrestling words. That view and all the lives it encompasses, domestic and wild, are the stuff of which my essays and stories are made—and my inspiration, my succor and surcease, my home. When I am stuck and the words don't come, I let my eyes wander from swallowtail butterflies cruising the beeplant to teenagers cruising the Safeway parking lot across the creek, and to cottony piles of cumulus clouds building over the valley in a promise of rain and renewed life for this perennially drought-parched landscape. Every detail holds a story, and those stories prime my work.

In the decade-plus since Richard and I moved to this place of his childhood hometown, tucked into a high-desert river valley in south-central Colorado, I have often asked him to just shoot me if I ever get used to this view. I mean it. I never want to take the landscape around me for granted. I hope to never be jaded by the surprising diversity of landforms, the complex tapestry of wild species and their interwoven relationships, the wild weather, and the friendly, frustrating, and fascinating human community.

Getting here—both to the place and the writing –required a long journey. Richard and I met twenty-five years ago in Laramie, Wyoming, where we were in graduate school. I had recently divorced myself from a marriage about which the less said the better; he was the devoted parent of Molly, a pre-schooler whose mother he had not yet divorced, but had been separated from for several years. To anybody who read the résumés, our past relationships didn't indicate that either of us would be good prospects for commitment, but we fell in love at first sight and it stuck.

We began a search for a place that would yield an academic job for Richard in a landscape I could call home. That quest took us back and forth across the country for the next decade and a half. Two days after our backyard marriage ceremony, we packed then four-year-old Molly and the most important of our belongings into our Subaru hatchback and headed for West Virginia, to Richard's first teaching appointment. We were back in Laramie the following summer, having lasted barely an academic year in the humid and verdant foothills of the Appalachians. In Laramie, we house-sat for Richard's major professor. Richard worked on his dissertation from a desk with an expansive view of prairie and the distant peaks of the Medicine Bow Range. At the end of the summer, he had hit an irreconcilable snag in his dissertation writing—view or no view—and we set off for Washington State, where we squeezed into my brother's crowded household while we hunted for work.

After three years of inhaling the salty tang of Puget Sound, wearing wool socks even in summer, and weathering Molly's discovery that slug slime will indeed numb your tongue, Richard's nearly finished doctorate called. We resigned our jobs, sold our tiny house tucked into a second-growth forest of still-adolescent western red cedar trees, and crammed our belongings into a U-Haul truck to move to Colorado.

A year, one completed dissertation, a publishing contract for my first book, and Molly's ninth birthday later, we packed up and moved again, this time with a larger rental truck, to Iowa, where Richard had a postdoctoral position at Iowa State University.

Two muggy Iowa summers, two tree-branch-breaking, ice-storm-punctuated winters, one book manuscript, and two Molly birthdays later, we moved again, this time to Las Cruces, New Mexico, where Richard joined the faculty of New Mexico State University.

Seven years later, during Molly's first year of college, and after I had written five more books, all about the desert region where we lived, I got homesick. I had gradually come to love the surprising verdancy revealed wherever the bare, sun-baked ground is blessed by water; the powerful spell of the hazy immensity of spare and sprawling basins punctuated by lizard-spined mountain ranges, the tarry smell of creosote bush, the melodic sound of Spanish everywhere, and the floods of spadefoot toads that emerge as if by magic from underground to call for mates in summer thunderstorms.

I wrote my way into knowing that landscape, as I had written my way into all the landscapes the three of us had inhabited since we left Wyoming: the dark hollows of West Virginia, Washington State's rain-drenched forests and saltwater bays, the sweeping rise of Colorado's Front Range, Iowa's fragments of once-endless prairie seas. I threw myself into learning each place, delving into geology, hydrology, and ecology in order to understand each landscape and its network of wild lives, and learning archeology, anthropology, and history to write the human story. I behaved as if belonging were a logical process, a matter of taking the right steps, just like science. Define the problem, collect the data, analyze the results, write it up and keep going until you've built up a body of knowledge, a relationship. But no matter how many research papers I read or experts I talked to, how much I learned or how many stories I wrote, none of those landscapes, even the surprising and magical desert, ever came to feel like home.

Still, I persisted. Although I sometimes succeeded in articulating what made each landscape unique and fascinating, writing what others said gave them the gift of seeing that place anew, kindling a connection they hadn't had before, in the end, my words failed to convince me. In fact, the more I learned and the more I wrote—the books, newspaper columns, radio commentaries, and magazine articles—the more I realized I didn't belong. In fact, I wrote myself out of each place. Eventually, reading what my writing did not say, what was not included, I began to understand that feeling at home is not a matter of proceeding step by step in a logical process. It is as much a matter of reading the metaphorical landscape of the heart as of learning the community of any literal land. When I was a child, I knew without a doubt where home was: Wyoming. Although my birth certificate and address placed me firmly in the state of Illinois, I recognized the home of my heart on a family vacation when I was still in grade school. It was June, the beginning of one of our annual marathon camping, hiking, and nature study expeditions through the West. My father was driving, gas pedal to the floor, urging the engine of our home-made camper-van to its top speed on the brand-new pavement of Interstate 80 somewhere west of Laramie. My mother, as chief navigator, sat in the seat next to him. My brother scanned the passing landscape for birds new to his life list. Ever the reader, I sat in back with my face buried in a book. As my father shifted down and we topped a hill, I looked up. Elk Mountain, still splotched with winter snow, rose out of the expanse of shrub desert like a massive ship, its prow pushing aside wave after wave of sagebrush, silver-green and spangled with spring moisture. Lupine exploded in purple flower spikes between the shrubs, and the air pouring in the open jalousie windows bore a fragrance I still find intoxicating: turpentine mixed with piney resin and the spicy sweetness of honey and orange blossoms.

*Sagebrush*, I said to myself. *I'm home.*

My heart swelled with feelings a child could not explain. I went back to my book. Not long after that, when an older lady at church asked me where I was from, I said, without hesitation, "Wyoming." My mother overheard my reply, and pulled me aside for an explanation. It was clear in my mind: I lived in Illinois during the school year, but home was the landscape my heart recognized, where sagebrush perfumed the air and mountains lined the horizon.

I moved to Wyoming after my second year in college, found a job in Yellowstone National Park, and returned to classes and textbooks as little as possible thereafter. I got my first job as a field ecologist in Wyoming, wrote my first scientific publications there, married for the first time, divorced, married more wisely the second time, wrote my first weekly newspaper column and left a career in science hoping to write the stories I could read in the data—all in the sparse and lonely landscapes of the state I called home. When Richard, Molly, and I drove out of Wyoming one August evening more than two decades ago, bound for West Virginia and his first faculty position, we stopped on a ridge with a view over the place we were leaving behind. I looked across that wide landscape of sagebrush and mountain range and cried as I said goodbye. It wasn't until many moves later, after attempting futilely to write each landscape where we lived into home, that I realized my childhood self had it wrong: it wasn't the state I loved, it was the shrub and the region it defines.

Scientists name the plant *Seriphidium tridentatum* subspecies *wyomingensis*, but most folks just call it big sage or more formally, Wyoming big sagebrush. Whatever the moniker, this gray-green shrub with the small, silver-hairy, three-tipped leaves (hence *tridentatum*) is the most common shrub in the inter-mountain West. Its gray-green foliage tints miles and miles of open landscape between the Rocky Mountains and the Sierra Nevada and Cascade ranges, from Canada south to northern Arizona. When rain hits these expanses of shrub desert, big sagebrush looses its signature fragrance on the air. One whiff of that distinctive scent, and I know I am home.

At nine, I didn't know why I loved sagebrush, just that something about it identified the place where I belonged. After I studied the plant as a scientist, I understood that big sage is so tightly woven into the landscapes where it grows that each defines the other. The shrub is supremely adapted to these wind-blown, arid, cold-winter places. Its three-tipped leaves are small and covered with an insulating felt of silver hairs to minimize water loss from the plant's cells, as well as to protect it from sun- and frost-burn. It retains those leaves year-round, photosynthesizing even on warm days in winter to compensate for their small size, which makes for less area to capture sunlight for food production. Its height and shape is tailored to the conditions of each site, ranging from knee-high and wind-pruned to eight feet tall. The shrub has even adapted its behavior: big sage actively reorients its leaves in response to the movements of sun and wind.

And it communicates. Legions of grazing creatures, from microscopic mites to half-ton ungulates are attracted to the shrub's evergreen foliage and succulent stems. Sagebrush protects itself by synthesizing the complex of chemicals that produce its signature fragrance, which, no matter how much I may love it, is not a sign of good taste—quite the opposite, in fact. The turpentine-like aromatic advertisement announces to grazers that the plant's tissues will taste bad and are gut-cloggingly difficult to digest. This ubiquitous shrub is as integral to these arid valleys and basins as pine and fir forests are to the adjacent mountains. The canopy of evenly spaced shrubs shades the ground like a dwarf forest overstory, protecting the surface from both searing daytime temperatures and frigid nights. It cuts the constant wind and retards evaporation from the soil. It traps airborne dust and detritus rich in organic matter and mineral nutrients. It captures rain, dripping the precious moisture into the ground slowly, and even collects its own mini-snowdrifts in winter to provide spring moisture. The shrub whose fragrance and form says "home" to me is in fact home to dozens of wildlife species, from pronghorn antelope and sagebrush lizard, to pygmy rabbit and sage-grouse.

When my homesickness for sagebrush country became acute, Richard had just been awarded tenure, the academic goal he had worked toward for so long. So I was stunned one evening when he proposed leaving that career behind to move to a landscape I could call home. He suggested his childhood hometown in south-central Colorado. Would that do? he asked. It had sagebrush, I said. Within weeks he had arranged for a leave of absence and we had sold our house. When Molly arrived home from college for the summer, we packed our belongings in the largest rental truck we could find and set out for a new life in a rural town a hundred miles from the nearest university (not to mention the nearest city, major airport, shopping mall, or interstate highway). Molly found a job at a local coffee shop; Richard took his formerly on-the-side consulting practice full time, and I worked on finishing my seventh book, the last, it turned out, about somewhere else.

The move did not go exactly as planned: the historic duplex we had bought required more work than we had imagined, from leaking roof and unsafe wiring to inoperable windows and spongy floors. As with all renovation projects, this one cost more and took longer than we expected, so we moved into a construction site, complete with the whine of power tools and work crews walking through our days. Our new space, while charming, totaled only 832 square feet, which made it a cozy fit for the two of us plus one very energetic dog. Molly lived next door. Richard's shop full of wood-and stone-working tools went into storage, along with some of our furniture. Eventually, we found the perfect shop for him, a sprawling and quite neglected brick building just across the alley from our duplex. It only required buying half a block of decaying industrial property choked in weeds and unwanted debris—and pursuing a lawsuit. We bought the place anyway, and Richard began making the shop building habitable in between trips for the consulting work that kept our finances afloat.

Two years after our move, it seemed finally as if we were settled. I had finished my first book set in our new region and was at work on a memoir about coming home. Richard resigned his faculty position. Not long afterward, his consulting work evaporated like drops of rain on a hot June sidewalk. He spent a winter working as a finish carpenter for the contractor who had remodeled our duplex, while I scrambled for writing assignments. The following year, the consulting work picked up again and we began building a house on our new parcel. We figured it would take about two years.

Six years later, we finally moved our stuff and our Great Dane across the alley. The house wasn't finished (who needs trim and cabinet doors?) but the consulting work was gone for good, and with it the income we had depended on. Still, I had finally written myself into home. Belonging came from the native bunchgrass prairie Richard and I lovingly restored on our formerly blighted site, from the abundance of the kitchen garden we raised to feed the two of us, and our neighbors, friends and families, and from the connections to the wider community, human, domestic, and wild, that we nurtured. Belonging gave my writing more than facts and stories. It acquired depth and heart, and the strength of purpose and tone that took my work to new levels and new audiences. Over time, that allowed Richard to pursue the work of his heart: abstract sculpture using native stone. His basins and sculptures bring rocks into our daily lives as ambassadors of the landscapes around us, and they inspire and inform my work.

What my heart recognized on that long-ago June day when Elk Mountain and spring-green sagebrush swam into my consciousness was that big sage belongs in these landscapes. It is as much at home as Richard's rocks, which shape the wide valleys and soaring peaks. The aromatic and abundant shrub is so tightly woven into this region that without it, these landscapes would indeed be as desolate—as deserted—as the deserts we call them. What I have learned from writing myself into this place, from the story of a shrub scientists call *Seriphidium tridentatum* is that being at home is not a logical process. It doesn't arise from a planned sequence of steps. No amount of learning alone can make a place home. It takes living, rooting as deeply as sagebrush, sprouting branches and leaves that cast shade and invite other lives to make themselves at home. It involves taking the place in, grain by grain and cell by cell, eating from its soil, inhaling its air, nurturing the wild community in your own yard and neighborhood, making the place a part of your daily life and your daily life a part of the place. I now understand that belonging means aspiring to contribute to this place I call home in ways as integral as big sagebrush, the plant of my heart, does to the whole region it defines.

And so I sit down to write at a desk full of stories built by my sculptor husband to fit into the bay of windows in my small office. Its table-like top is formed of practical laminate in a pattern that echoes brushed steel reminiscent of the industrial history of this site. The frame is of white ash, wood that may have come from Arkansas, the state where Richard, who gave me the gift of this landscape, was born a year before his family moved to a house a few blocks from this one. It is also the state where the river that rushes close enough by that we sometimes hear it at night meets the Mississippi. The smooth, chocolate brown mesquite pegs that hold the mortise-and-tenon joints of my desk together come from the deserts of southwest Texas, near where Richard lived after his family left Colorado and near where he and I and Molly lived before we returned here. The drawer pulls are flattened pebbles that we selected from a beach in Oregon. A sprig of sagebrush snipped from the shrubs dotting our yard sits in a small vase on the shelf next to me. I smile as I think of the myriad stories woven together to shape this desk, this landscape, and this thing we call life. I lift my eyes to the windows to trace the undulating skyline of my home, east to west, sunrise to sunset. And then I put fingers to keyboard and begin to write.

**Joe Stone** writes from his home in Salida where the sound of the Arkansas River resonates through the open window of his office. Joe holds bachelor's and master's degrees in English from Texas A&M and the University of Tennessee, respectively. He served as a technical writer for the Oak Ridge National Laboratory for eight years. Since returning to Colorado, he has transitioned into a freelance writer for regional and on-line publications, editing books and magazines, and designing web sites.

Fascinated by the universality of spiritual truth across belief systems, Stone has studied the teachings of Christianity, Pagan, Hindu, Taoist, Buddhist, and various indigenous belief systems. Now a shamanic priest, Joe writes with clarity and purpose about the most important questions of our time.

# The Writer as Shaman

## Joe Stone

> ...and the Word was with God, and the Word was God.
> He was with God in the beginning.
> Through Him all things were created.
> —John 1:1–3

MY CAREER AS a writer began straight out of college. Having studied the greatest literary works of the English language, I entered the mundane white-collar world of technical writing. Seven years in the rarified air of academia had opened my eyes to transcendent realms of thought and inspired creativity, but the reality of supporting a family took precedence over my dreams of returning to the Colorado mountains to write creatively. I soon found myself driving two hours each day to stare at a tiny monochrome computer screen and write government proposals for things like "vehicle operation, maintenance and analysis services"— not exactly my idea of a dream job.

After a year I accepted a job with better pay and benefits at Oak Ridge National Laboratory. The largest of our national labs, Oak Ridge is also home to the world's first nuclear reactor, which claims the dubious distinction of dual listing on the National Register of Historic Places and as a Superfund cleanup site. For six years, I edited documents about a wide range of environmental issues—incineration of chemical weapons, radioactive isotopes in groundwater, mercury in surface water, nuclear power plants, greenhouse gas emissions, hydroelectric power. For eight to ten hours a day, five days a week, I sat in a cubicle where I sifted through pages of scientific information, editing it into the comprehensible sentences and paragraphs that filled environmental reports up to two thousand pages long. I did good work, I advanced to the top of my job family, and then I burned out.

Focused on meeting the physical needs of a young family, I got caught up in society's materialist system and lost touch with my dreams. I lost touch with the Creative Source of artistic expression. I still sensed that transcendent source, especially on long hikes into the lush forests near my Smoky Mountain home, but I had convinced myself to invest my energies in the technocratic system of our rational materialist culture. By the time I received my layoff notice, my marriage had entered the early stages of divorce. My rational world of work and family dissolved into a sea of grief and despair. Marriage counseling and freelance work only prolonged the inevitable, and with nothing more than a Toyota pickup and an empty bank account, I finally moved back to Colorado to work for an old friend.

I worked in Denver for a year, helping my friend manage a small telecom company, before taking a job as an electrician and project manager at a small engineering firm. I was still stuck in a production-oriented, technology-driven workplace, but at least I was back in the mountains where I could eat my lunch on a sunny boulder, take hikes along shady streams and enjoy the views from mountain peaks. The natural beauty of the Rocky Mountains eased the tension and refreshed my soul. I avoided distractions like dating and television for several years. I lived a contemplative life, and I slowly rediscovered my dreams and myself. I remembered that writing was my true calling, my purpose in life.

I made the transition into freelance writing much sooner than expected; at the same time, I entered an extended period of personal growth. At every step, I experienced epiphanies and synchronicities—unexplainable coincidences that provided exactly the opportunities I needed exactly when I needed them. The more I paid attention to the synchronicities, the more readily life flowed. The less I struggled to meet the material demands of life, the more readily my needs were met. The more deeply I delved into my own identity, the more readily I recognized and embraced the unconscious aspects of the psyche. The most powerful (and completely unexpected) synchronicities that

I experienced during this time culminated in my initiation into a shamanic spiritual tradition. Shamanic initiation purports to transform the initiate from a profane human condition to a sacred one. For me, the experience reached beyond what words can express and filled me with a deep sense of peace.

While most of us have a general understanding of shamanism as a type of tribal spirituality, it runs counter to our culture's secular materialist mindset. But the shaman plays a crucial role in the so-called "primitive" cultures, acting as a healer and an intermediary between society and the supernatural. In Jungian terms, the shaman functions as society's liaison to the archetypal symbols of the collective unconscious, bringing the members of his society into close contact with these archetypes. He fulfills this intermediary role by performing shamanic rituals and narrating mythic stories that illuminate the archetypes and inform the culture. By reaffirming the universal symbols, the shaman ensures that society recognizes and honors the fundamental aspects of the psyche that exist in the mystical realms beyond ordinary consciousness. The shaman does more, however, than just recite the myths or enact the rituals of religious symbolism. He lives the myth, existing outside the social norm—on the fringes of society and the edges of "normal" consciousness.

Our cultural mindset sees shamanism, with its myths and mysticism, as outdated and superstitious. Meanwhile, armed with the technological achievements of science, this same mindset produced and perpetuates unsustainable trends—mass consumption, environmental destruction, political violence and weapons production, including weapons of mass destruction. Nonetheless, the rational materialist view continues to dominate, insisting that scientific reason and objectivity can explain all things. Unfortunately, science's compartmentalized observations repeatedly fail to see the bigger picture. Invariably, the scientific solution produces unexpected side effects that cause unprecedented types of problems. Science presumes to solve the new problems only to produce more side effects and complications. If science produces the problems, can we really put our faith in science to solve the problems?

Of all the scientific disciplines, quantum physics provides the most intriguing information about our human dilemma. In observing the fundamental elements of physical reality, quantum physicists tell us that perception alters physical reality. In other words, science's hallowed position of objectivity does not exist. Anyone who observes this universe participates in the universe and experiences it subjectively, co-creating physical reality through the act of perceiving it. It works something like this: everything at the subatomic level is comprised of energy waves of possibility. Consciousness collapses these waves into particles of matter, ultimately creating our physical reality. The implications are huge. In fact, each human being, as a locus of consciousness, is ultimately responsible for co-creating the world in which we live. Reality is based on consciousness, not matter.

Interestingly, Eastern traditions, particularly Hinduism, have long held to the same basic concept of reality, regarding the material world as Maya, an illusion. In essence, each human being is a single drop of water on the vast ocean of consciousness, and Maya is the dualistic realm of the five senses, the physical "reality" that barely skims the surface of this limitless ocean. The path to enlightenment leads beyond the surface illusion of Maya into the depths of consciousness, the transcendent realm beyond duality. Given the illusory nature of physical existence, the only way to attain enlightenment is by personally experiencing the transcendent level of consciousness. Focusing on the dualistic reality of Maya (the material universe) perpetuates the unenlightened consciousness dominated by the ego and its false dichotomy of the self separate from the rest of the universe.

This essential concept, that the universe consists of various levels of consciousness, points to a worldview known as the "perennial philosophy" because it appears and reappears across diverse cultures throughout human history. In fact, the perennial philosophy has formed the core of the world's major wisdom traditions as well as the teachings of the greatest philosophers, scientists and psychologists. Regardless of the tradition, the language or the age, the essential elements of the perennial philosophy find expression with such persistence as to suggest that it is humanity's most accurate reflection of reality. Since the ultimate, transcendent reality of the perennial philosophy lies beyond the range of ego consciousness, it cannot be expressed through language. To know this ultimate reality requires the internal act of a contemplative practice that transcends words and ego, allowing the experience of the Creative Source of the Divine. The writings and teachings of those who experienced this reality, whether Hindu, Christian, Buddhist, Muslim, Hebrew or Taoist, all point to the same, indescribable Truth.

Central to the perennial philosophy is the concept of the Great Chain of Being, which describes a reality composed of several dimensions or levels of being from the least conscious to total consciousness. At the least conscious end of this spectrum, we find the inanimate objects of physical matter. The transcendent end of the spectrum is described by words like "spirit," "godhead" and "superconscious" and is the Creative Source from which all the other levels come into being. Perhaps the best-known proponent of this worldview, Aldous Huxley describes the four doctrines fundamental to the perennial philosophy in his introduction to the *Bhagavad-Gita* translated by Swami Prabhavananda and Christopher Isherwood.

> First: the phenomenal world of matter and of individualized consciousness—the world of things and animals and men and even gods—is the manifestation of a Divine Ground within which all partial realities have their being, and apart from which they would be non-existent.
>
> Second: human beings are capable not merely of knowing *about* the Divine Ground by inference; they can also realize its existence by a direct intuition, superior to discursive reasoning. This immediate knowledge unites the knower with that which is known.
>
> Third: man possesses a double nature, a phenomenal ego and an eternal Self, which is the inner man, the spirit, the spark of divinity within the soul. It is possible for a man, if he so desires, to identify himself

with the spirit and therefore with the Divine Ground, which is of the same or like nature with the spirit.

Fourth: man's life on earth has only one end and purpose: to identify himself with his eternal Self and so to come to unitive knowledge of the Divine Ground.

If the purpose of life is union with the Divine Source of creation, the basic problem is how to gain this "immediate knowledge" that "unites the knower with that which is known." This involves the internal work of recognizing the ego's limiting influences and moving beyond those limitations to identify with the Self and reunite with the Divine level of consciousness. Unfortunately, we must overcome a cultural worldview that sees the material illusion of Maya as the ultimate reality. Science describes human beings as accidents of natural selection in a universe without meaning. Caught up in this limited level of reality, we have lost our sense of unity with the cosmos as well as our awareness of the divine spark within, and society's self-destructive trends accelerate unchecked. These are exactly the conditions that could benefit from the influence of shamanic figures, individuals who can maintain the reality of the Divine within themselves and reacquaint the members of society with their own Divine nature.

As Huxley implies, the primary barrier to this process is the human ego. With its incessant, babbling thoughts—the continuous internal monologue that compares, judges, speculates, complains and so on—the ego controls our consciousness and prevents us from achieving the quiet, contemplative state required to enter the deeper levels of consciousness. Carl Jung referred to these deeper levels as the collective unconscious, the domain of the mythic archetypes, and described a process of "individuation" whereby the ego's dominant position is subordinated so that the psyche can interact with the archetypes and reconnect with the Divine. (Interestingly, Jung first viewed this process as an initiatory privilege of the shaman.)

Almost any type of contemplative practice can help move us beyond ego and into the individuation process—meditation, fly fishing, Contemplative Prayer, needlepoint, Tai Chi, journaling. By quieting the ego's incessant thought-noise, we begin to free ourselves from the limits of the ego-based identity. We begin to observe the ego's thoughts, and in so doing, we broaden our consciousness beyond ego. From a contemplative place, we can also begin to observe our emotions and recognize that, like the ego's thoughts, emotions are simply another aspect of a limited level of consciousness. As we begin to free ourselves from the ego's false identity of thoughts intertwined with emotions, we are ready to begin the "quest perilous" into the deeper levels of the psyche.

The most fearful step is confronting the shadow—the archetypal gatekeeper and guardian of the nether realm, the black knight who says, "Thou shall not pass" into the deeper levels of consciousness. The shadow represents those aspects of ourselves that we dislike, the parts that the ego prefers to avoid through repression and projection. But in order to go deeper, we must confront the shadow and integrate it into our consciousness; otherwise, we allow the ego to project these negative aspects of ourselves onto others and avoid accepting the true source of the negativity within ourselves. Once we have successfully integrated the negative aspects of the shadow, we free ourselves to access the deeper levels of consciousness.

Having survived the fearful confrontation with the shadow, we have passed into the unknown territory of the unconscious. But if we know the mythic stories, we can recognize that we have embarked upon the great heroic journey, and we can read the mythological symbols recorded by those who have passed this way before us. Men enter the unknown territory in search of the beautiful princess, imprisoned against her will. The princess symbolizes *anima*, man's inner feminine and the muse who connects him to his creativity, thereby empowering him for the ultimate quest, to seek the Holy Grail, the Divine essence of himself. For women, it is the journey of Isis seeking out the body of her dead husband so that he may be brought back to life, bringing into consciousness the *animus*, the unrecognized masculine aspects of herself. Completing the symbolic journey requires an encounter with the wise old man or woman, who points the way to the discovery of the priceless treasure at the deepest levels of consciousness, where each of us can, in Huxley's words, "identify himself with his eternal Self and so to come to unitive knowledge of the Divine Ground."

But the unitive knowledge of enlightenment is absent from our contemporary worldview, and science's technology, its poisonous by-products and weapons of mass destruction are projections of the human psyche, expressions of our limited level of consciousness. From this perspective, science is simply a manifestation of the ego seeking to assuage its fear of death by exerting control over nature (instead of seeing ourselves as a part of nature and putting ourselves in accord with nature). The negative effects and unforeseen consequences that accompany technological progress are the nightmarish projections of the collective psyche's shadow elements. "Look at the devilish engines of destruction!" Jung wrote in *Psychology and Religion: West and East*. "They are invented by completely innocuous gentlemen, reasonable, respectable citizens who are everything we could wish. And when the whole thing blows up, and an indescribable hell of destruction is let loose, nobody seems responsible. It simply happens, and yet it is all man-made."

Joseph Campbell recognized our cultural dilemma. "We've lost the symbols," he said in *Sukhavati: A Mythic Journey*.

> Meanwhile, we need the symbols, and they come up in disturbed dreams and nightmares and so forth, which are dealt with by the psychiatrist. It was with Freud and Jung and Adler that it was realized, and particularly through Jung, that the figures of dreams are really figures of personal mythologization. You're creating your own imagery related to the archetypes. But the culture has rejected them. The culture has gone into an economic and political phase where the spiritual principles are completely disregarded. The religious life is ethical; it is not mystical. That is gone, and the society is disintegrating consequently.

Society needs to reconnect with the symbols of mythology, the symbols of the collective unconscious. And this is the role of the true shaman, to reconnect the members of his society with the archetypes of the collective unconscious, initiating each human being into his or her own mythic journey of Self-discovery. Having made the archetypal journey himself, the shaman is conscious of his true identity and can, therefore, remind the rest of us that we can be united with the Divine Ground, the deepest and the highest level of consciousness. But, Daniel Pinchbeck says in *2012: The Return of Quetzacoatl:*

> From a shamanic perspective, the psychic blockade that prevents otherwise intelligent adults from considering the future of our world—our obvious lack of future, if we continue on our present path—reveals an occult dimension. It is like a programming error written into the software designed for the modern mind, which has endless energy to expend on the trivial and treacly, sports statistics or shoe sale, but no time to spare for the torments of the Third World, for the mass extinction of species to perpetuate a way of life without a future, for the imminent exhaustion of fossil fuels, or for the fine print of the Patriot Act. This psychic blockade is reinforced by a vast propaganda machine spewing out crude as well as sophisticated distractions, encouraging individuals to see themselves as alienated spectators of their culture, rather than active participants in a planetary ecology.

Or, as Campbell put it, "There's no conflict between mysticism and science, but there is a conflict between the science of 2000 B.C. and the science of 2000 A.D. and that's the mess in our religions. We've got stuck with an image of the universe that's about as simple and childish as you can imagine... It's of no use to us. We have to have *poets* ... who will render to us the experience of the transcendent through the world in which we're living." Naturally, the modern shaman needs some means of fulfilling his intermediary role between society and the transcendent, and Campbell recognized that the poets, the inspired writers, are the ones who can narrate the mythic stories that illuminate the archetypes and inform the culture, rendering to society "the experience of the transcendent through the world in which we're living."

In this world in which we live, we experience the transcendent in moments of synchronicity, paradox, epiphany, etc. During those transcendent moments, creativity breaks through the barriers of the ego and allows a greater awareness to inform our consciousness. These are the experiences that the shaman works to induce. This is also the experience of inspired writing—true creativity flowing from the Creative Source, the Divine Ground. As the writer's consciousness becomes more closely connected to the Creative Source of the transcendent, the ego's barriers begin to dissolve, and he becomes increasingly aware of the alignment of forces within the psyche, the archetypes of the collective unconscious. The energy of these internal forces of consciousness produces an external resonance that propagates outward into the world energetically, like quantum energy waves of possibility that manifest the transcendent into the physical particles of our material universe.

Drawing on these shamanic energies, the writer invests the archetypal symbols and myths with new power to inform humanity in *this* world, today's world. On the one hand, these resonant energies subtly raise the consciousness of humanity as a whole. On the other hand, the more writer-poets who render the transcendent into the external world, the more we enhance human consciousness and the closer we come to a transformation of consciousness, a higher level of being. Could such a transformation reflect the "end of time" described by so many spiritual traditions? Apocalypse comes from the Greek root *apokalyptein*, which means, "to uncover." By uncovering the deeper levels of consciousness hidden by the ego's superficialities, perhaps we are preparing the way for a total transformation of consciousness that will dissolve our rational ideas about objectivity and causality and manifest a reality defined by spontaneity, synchronicity and creativity. "Without effort, one world moves into another," states a passage in the *Rig Veda*.

From the Jungian perspective, the Apocalypse is an archetype, representing aspects of the collective psyche. Jung's follower, Edward Edinger, considered the Apocalypse to be a profound psychological event that represented the coming of the Self into conscious realization.

For Edinger, the collective individuation of humanity advances through the course of human history, and the end result of that process, the "coming of the Self," is now imminent. According to Edinger this process of reintegrating humanity into a unified entity is inevitable, but the outcome is not. If human beings choose to remain caught up in their individual ego identities and the material illusion of Maya, humanity will be unified in an Armageddon of mutual mass destruction. But if a sufficient number of individuals can manifest the coming of the Self as an individual, inner experience, we can achieve unity by means of mutual human consciousness and be spared the worst features of the external manifestation of Apocalypse.

In *The Gospel of Thomas*, Christ's words affirm Edinger's vision: "If you bring forth what is within you, what you bring forth will save you. If you do not bring forth what is within you, what you do not bring forth will destroy you." We can witness on the nightly news the destruction that our repressed shadows project into the world, but the process that offers salvation starts within each individual. The ego's domination of the psyche must be ended through individuation. Only then, as a fully self-reflective individual consciousness can one freely make the choice to reconcile with the Divine, sacrificing the false self of the ego. The core of our human struggle has been recorded in the ancient myths, providing us with the roadmap of the human psyche that can help show us The Way out of the illusion of Maya and into the transcendent level of being. Contemporary writers, fluent in the mythic language of symbols, are uniquely positioned to glean the archetypal kernels of Truth from these myths and translate them into intelligible modern concepts, thereby performing the shamanic functions that inform society of the deeper levels of consciousness. Society desperately needs shamanic writers, human beings who have ventured into different realms of consciousness, who live the myths and can convey to society the limitless possibilities of an enlightened consciousness.

The shamanic writer must live in the present, pursuing dreams and inspirations, the private mythology that leads down his unique path into the mythic world of archetypes. Ultimately, the transcendent manifests as a personal mystical experience that can never be fully communicated. As such, the shaman, having experienced the transcendent levels of consciousness, can only describe the path to transcendence through the symbolic communication of myth. As Joseph Campbell said, "The passage is from dream to vision to the Gods, and they are you. All the Gods, all the Heavens, all the Hells are within you. The God is in you. It is not something that happened somewhere else a long time ago. It's in you. This is the truth of truths. This is what the Gods and myths are all about, so find them in yourself and take them into yourself and you will be awakened in your mythology and in your life."

Something compels me to write. Something compels me to live outside the confines of "normal" society. Something compels me search the darkest realms of the psyche as well as the brightest light in the heavens and the most serene moments in nature. And we all know that the world cannot continue on its present course indefinitely. A fundamental shift must occur, and time moves exponentially now. The river quickens as it approaches the falls. The ravings of a lunatic or the flashes of vision into transcendent levels of consciousness … how do you render the experience of the transcendent without a trace of lunacy?

The shaman performs his rituals, works his magic, within the sacred space of the circle. And so I close this circle, ending with the beginning and knowing that, within the circle scribed by these words, I have worked my magic, the creation rites of the Word, to bring you into close contact with the mystical world of the mythic symbols, encouraging you into a deeper realm of consciousness, even if only for a moment. And the energy waves of possibility you generate by contemplating these words resonates into the world and brings us that much closer to the new reality of unitive consciousness.

In the beginning was the Word…

When she is not hiking in the high country or on the road presenting workshops, poet, novelist, and memoirist **Laurie Wagner Buyer** divides her time between Woodland Park, Colorado, and Llano, Texas. Laurie has an MFA in Writing from Goddard College in Vermont, and is the author of five collections of poetry: *Glass-Eyed Paint in the Rain*, *Red Colt Canyon*, *Infinite Possibilities: A Haiku Journal*, *Accidental Voices* and *Across the High Divide*. The latter won the Western Writers of America Spur Award in Poetry and was named a Willa Cather Literary Award finalist. Five Star, an imprint of Thomson-Gale, released her first novel *Side Canyons*. Laurie received the Beryl Markham Prize for *Spring's Edge: A Ranch Wife's Chronicles*, a memoir published in 2008 by the University of New Mexico Press. A second memoir about living in the Montana wilderness, *When I Came West*, was released by the University of Oklahoma Press in 2010. Laurie's freelance articles, poems, and photographs have appeared in dozens of periodicals, journals, reviews, and anthologies.

# An Elevated View

### Laurie Wagner Buyer

> "Roads are almost everywhere. Often times we deceive ourselves and think we are much more remote than we actually are. All it takes to realize this is an elevated view."—Bill Worrell, *Voices from the Cave*

NO MATTER WHERE I walked from the old log house, the Colorado landscape demanded that I go up. The homestead era building with mudsill foundation leaned into the earth at the lowest elevation on the ranch. Tall willows and ancient spruce trees guarded the hand-hewn walls. A side channel of the river ran a stone's throw away. There the beaver loved to build dams so that a small pond often graced the view out the long kitchen window from which I gazed while washing dishes. From waterways to meadows to sage-studded pastures to an array of ridges, the South Fork of the South Platte valley rose to greater and greater heights: Black Mountain, Round Mountain, Buffalo Peaks, the far-off Tarryalls, and the forbidding fourteeners of the Mosquito Range. No matter where I looked, mountains challenged my view.

I had grown up with much different horizons. Air Force base quarters in the Philippines and Hawaii offered sea level, tropical forest vistas. Civilian housing in Little Rock, Minot, and San Antonio proffered different degrees of flat plains or rolling hills. Backwoods environs near Glacier National Park and ranch life on the Upper Green River held spectacular ranges like the Sawtooths, the Bridgers, and the Wind Rivers, but those mountains existed so distant from my everyday life that they served more as postcard reveries than true influences.

In Colorado I came face to face with actual elevation on a daily basis. The ranch house hunkered down at 9,600 feet and everything else was a continuous climb upward. Even the driveway leading out to the county road maintained a stubborn two-tenths of a mile steady upgrade. Whenever I walked, the landscape insisted on engaging lungs and legs in the pursuit of expanding endurance. Altitude, as well as attitude, became a constant in-my-face reality.

I begrudged Colorado that first summer of 1988. We lived in a wall tent and slept on cots. We cooked canned food and had no way to shower. We hauled water in gallon jugs from a spring and I washed clothes by hand. We fought packrats and mice and porcupines. We strung wire in unforgiving sun and set posts in stony ground with little topsoil. When I complained to an older neighboring ranch woman she reminded me, "That's why we call it the 'Rocky Mountains.'" The hellacious wind never stopped blowing and frost coated the tent roof even in July. Still, wildflowers bloomed in splendid disarray, choirs of coyotes yowled from the ridges, elk arrived to graze nearby, jays, ravens, and magpies became daily visitors, and owls called out the night hours. The morning I spotted my first unbelievably orange Rocky Mountain lily in the mushy ground along the spring runnel where I bent to dip a coffee pot full of water, I began to believe that Colorado might have enough delicate beauty and fragile grace to save me from the despair of having to learn yet another new landscape.

Making friends with a place had never been easy for me. A shy and awkward girl, I seldom managed to get my feet beneath me before the balance of life shifted. Shuffled from place to place whenever my father transferred to a different military base, I attended fourteen schools in twelve years, and then went on to three colleges. By the time I was thirty-four, I had moved twenty-eight times. Only once, when I decided to come West from Chicago in 1975, had the choice been totally mine. Otherwise, my father, societal and educational expectations, and male partners dictated my moves. While my resistant spirit begged to stay put and set down permanent roots somewhere, my heart succumbed to the attachment of person instead of place. Repeatedly, I faced the uneasy task of convincing new landscapes that I could be a worthy inhabitant. In Colorado this meant I either learned to climb to greater heights or I failed the ultimate test of belonging.

My husband at the time had been raised on the rarified air near Fairplay. So had his parents and grandparents. He carried three generations worth of knowing the land in his blood. Inherent toughness triggered his confident steps. Though in his sixties, he had the athletic heart of a thirty-year-old. Though his knees were riddled with arthritis he walked and climbed like a billy goat, and he never took the well-worn path. He preferred bucking brush and exploring the steepest ravines. In contrast, I huffed and puffed and cussed. My younger heart thrashed against my ribs as my legs turned to jelly. It was not uncommon for me to collapse in a pathetic, white-faced shaking heap pleading, "I just want to go home," even though I had no idea where that was or what that meant. The mountains, in their eternal, stoic indifference, did not care.

I grew weaker. I fell ill. The landscape said, "Get tough or die." I could not walk from the house to the barn, much less to the county road. In my anguish and my inability to understand what was happening to me, I wrote with tears plopping on the page. Why had I been brought to this foreboding place? Why was everything so difficult? Why couldn't I adjust to this new environment? Why wouldn't Colorado befriend me? Wasn't I trying hard enough? Was there some sacrifice I had to make in order to belong? Maybe I was meant to die.

In desperation, I turned to the river, the sky, the birds, the animals, the trees and the rocks. On my daily treks for water, I lay down on my belly in the muck to talk to the seep-spring monkey flowers. When I threw out the dirty dishwater, I spoke to the gophers that poked curious heads out of myriad holes. When cow elk barked, I answered with my best imitation of a wandering calf. I purchased books to identify the plants and trees. I searched for arrowheads and antlers. And I wrote. I filled legal pads with observations, questions, and unrelenting affirmations to ward off loneliness and despair.

When a woman has no one to talk to, she talks to herself. When a writer has no audience, she writes for herself. It did not matter that no one would ever read the brilliant lines of anguish splashed across my pages. What mattered was that I fought to get the arguments out of my head and the emotions out of my heart in order to alleviate the pain manifesting in my muscles and joints. Any writer who says they do not write for therapy has to be fibbing. I wrote because I had to, because the process released inner stress, because the words allowed me an escape from my usual world, and because scribbling made me feel better. And at the end of every day, if I had nothing else to show for the hours I spent using up precious oxygen, I had journal notes. When nothing came to mind to occupy my pen, I copied recipes from cookbooks or wrote letters to friends. The positive action of moving a pen across a piece of paper became my proof that I still functioned even if at the rate of slime mold.

While I went through the usual rounds of doctors and tests, attempted diet changes and psychotherapy, courted angels and wrestled with demons, I documented my journey in precise detail. And I walked. I exhaled anxiety and fear, and inhaled the thin air like elixir. Despite my frail state of battling pernicious anemia, each day I pushed myself to go a bit farther, to climb a little higher. On the evening that I made it up the driveway to the county road, I burst into tears when I touched the gate like a goal post. The dog licked my hand and whined. The ascending ridges and mountains stared down at me with consummate disregard. Two hundred feet? That's nothing. Try four thousand more. It reminded me of publishing my first freelance article only to be chided, "When are you going to write a book?"

Copper Ridge provided my next challenge. Though I knew I could not make the mile and a half to the top, I chose a lone ponderosa pine on the gradually rising flat as my target. Every day I pushed forty or fifty paces closer to the old sentinel. When I finally made the tree's acquaintance by hugging close the rough bark, I heard a female voice murmur, "Good for you." I named her the grandmother tree and graced her branches with queries and prayers. The wind that moved through the needles encouraged me onward. As fall settled into winter, I followed the tracks of elk up the narrow, stony path into groves of gold-leaved aspen and denser, darker woods. Here nighthawks traced my movement with screeching cries, "She's coming. She's coming."

Weeks later, when I finally made the summit, I found a gnarled mate to the ponderosa far below. I named him the grandfather tree and gripped one of his outstretched broken branches in both hands to attempt wimpy chin-ups. Not far from the pine's base I found a flat stone on which to sit and recapture my breath. From here I could see far south to the rounded formation of Buffalo Peaks. If I followed the hogback east, the game trail brought me to a high point overlooking the ranch meadows with their winding silver ribbon of river. The buildings looked like dollhouses, the vehicles and equipment like Tonka toys, the horses like tiny black dashes. On the exposed outcropping the wind swirled old stories. Who else had stood here to take in the view? Who had picked and sweated and shoveled out the rocks to find the traces of green-laced copper? Who had chipped the flint pieces and left the broken arrowheads? Knowing that others before me had left some small trace of existence soothed my spirit. If I resurrected some of those stories would a publisher be interested? *The Fence Post* began to print my poems and articles and photographs, and as my file of clippings grew I gained name recognition and acceptance into the cowboy poetry community.

Seasons turned into years. I climbed Copper Ridge. The financially strapped ranch threatened to go under so I took a job in town. Still, before work each day, I climbed Copper Ridge. While I snarled at the wolves at the ranch house door and growled at the health problems that still trailed my heels, I continued to find time to stop and chat with the grandmother tree and the grandfather tree. When my father was diagnosed with esophageal cancer the same spring that my first book was nominated for the Colorado Book Award, I chugged up Copper Ridge to offer pleas for his healing along with prayers of gratitude. My constant tracks intermingled with those of deer and elk, and coyotes. My frustrated, tired tears splashed the flat rock when I knew I dared not sit down to rest for fear I could not get back up. Though I could not bear to stare at the unreachable high peaks, the ever-changing beauty of the ridges and the ever-flowing current of the river gave me reason to go on.

I learned that I could not write a poem without crafting a line, and I could not vision a line without the words connected to image, and I could not gather images without experience. The omnipresent need to write drove me outdoors even in the worst weather. I did not carry a notebook or pen, nor did I ever venture out with some preplanned notion of what I might return with. Instead, I traveled blind through snowstorms, deafened by yowling winds. I grew to love those rare moments caught between two lights, dawn and dusk, sunrise and sunset, moonshine and star sparkle, full moon and no moon. Even in the darkest hours of the night, I sometimes slipped outside to walk my well-worn trail with only foot feel to find my way, with the ghost-white dog returning every few moments to touch his nose to my hand. If there were answers out there somewhere, surely I would come across them eventually. If only I could climb high enough, perhaps I might be able to spot the right trail, see some set of ruts that would show me the way. Lost in the strange, confused landscape of the heart, I did not want to panic. I did not want to be trapped forever in a room where I battered myself against the illuminated, but closed windows because I could not see the wide open door. Because I believed an exit existed, because I believed I could find it, I never stopped searching. I sought help from healers, read countless books for enlightenment, and wrote about each new agony that gripped my spirit.

My father's death released me from the fear that I would lose him. When he chose hospice over hope of recovery I began the slow process of letting go. His final wishes for me granted me permission to create my own future. He asked me to publish a children's story I had written that he loved, and he asked me to go back to school for a master's degree. Honoring his requests forced me to leave the now comfortable domain of the ranch with its precise boundaries, known territory, and close community of neighbors. Reaching an elevated place no longer meant climbing Copper Ridge. The new challenge required broader horizons, a wide-angle view, an all-embracing mind and a fear-free heart.

The converted dairy farm campus of Goddard College in Vermont led me to the Grand Canyon. Any map will illustrate that convoluted route, yet inevitable connections lay waiting at every turn of the trail. In my writing and in my life, I began to believe in synchronicity. I began to understand that intimacy with landscape existed everywhere. Whether engaged in a one-night stand, a day's outing, a weeklong retreat, a month of wandering, an extended love affair, or a lifetime commitment to one place, the images gathered and the words garnered created the stories that sustained me.

On the page I could depict reality, craft fantasy, develop plots, reveal people, invent characters, save lives, ruin lives, break and mend hearts, become a genius or admit to being narcissistic. On the page my husband and I solved our problems, the ranch was saved, the calves never died, my father lived forever, my enemies adored me, and my friends never deserted me. I discovered the alchemy of mixing place with purpose, the power of allowing life, and therefore the written word, to be whatever it wanted to be. And I learned that finding answers to important questions, like why do you write, invariably led to more complicated questions, like: Why do you want to leave your husband? Why can't you get well?

On the Colorado River in the Grand Canyon I found answers and spotted exit signs everywhere. The ancient ones had left directions hand-painted or etched on cliff walls and in caves. They had climbed to high places for the elevated view. Where our goat-footed trip leader led, I followed with sweaty palms. Though invisible to others, I saw arrows pointing up, down, left, right, and in each cardinal direction. Rock, sky, campfire, and river called out to me. All I had to do was choose. Why stay in one spot when I could go anywhere on earth? Why remain in a suffocating emotional morass when relief could be found with one breath of fresh air? Why allow fear to hold up interminable caution lights and stop signs when the signal fire burned bright? Why crawl on hands and knees when the giant current offered easy passage?

I did not come home healed. Instead, I returned to the Colorado ranch stronger and more determined. Though I continued to hold the place in reverence, Copper Ridge held no allure. I turned south to the forested ridge that shielded Jones Hill and the Buffalo Peaks Wilderness

Area beyond. I rode horseback across Long Park and up Rough and Tumble Creek. On the days that I walked, I scaled the small round mound of Bull Elk hill where I could turn a circle and see 360 degrees. Roads, hiking paths, and game trails stretched in all directions. I became aware of rabbit routes through the brush and mouse mazes through the grass. Along the top of the ridge that led from the creek to Bull Elk hill, the timber fell away to leave an exposed crest. I longed to run for the sheer joy of movement, but hesitated. Though seasons of walking and climbing had strengthened my legs and my lungs, I had not run or jogged for twenty years. Would my forty-five year old body remember what to do?

I bounced up and down in place to test my calves and heels. I danced back and forth to feel the unevenness of the stony ground. There was no one to see me fail, no one to notice if I only made a hundred feet before I quit. The crest rested flat and trackless in front of me before a narrow trail appeared to dip down a gully and emerge on the other side. What could it hurt? I forced the image of a sprained ankle or broken leg out of my mind. Instead, I focused on the shimmering lemon-gold grass atop Bull Elk hill. Like the lone ponderosa pine I named the grandmother tree that rounded apex became my new goal.

When I shifted from fast walk to shuffling jog, my hips and knees cried out at the impact, but my shoulders, arms, and spine relaxed into the motion. I smiled. My body remembered. I increased my pace in increments as my legs fell into the old pattern and found the right rhythm. Now my lungs squeaked. I sucked in the high altitude air with short fast gasps. My heart tripped over itself trying to keep pace. The stitch in my left side threatened to rip apart. The trail leading into the gully came into closer view. I pounded toward it, fighting widespread cellular pain. My hands turned numb and my head throbbed as blood pumped through arteries and pushed against resistant veins. A few more steps, a few more paces, and then I sailed over the edge and scrambled for footing going down, down, my feet flying, my arms flailing for balance. I was running. I was running! For the first time in two decades, I was running.

I stumbled up the other side of the gully and ran on, slower now, with even steps, the breath flowing in and out of my lungs like a well-oiled bellows. I had broken through some invisible barrier to some sort of otherworldly zone, to a place of effortless bliss where everything was easy and uncomplicated. How had I forgotten the peace and comfort of that perfect space within? I had searched for years, and then found the answer with that one gargantuan physical push outward into rebirth. Or as my father had confessed to me before he lapsed into unconsciousness the last time, "Dying is easy. All you have to do is let go."

Bull Elk hill glistened another quarter mile away. I ran out of energy and air. I slowed again to a jog, then a walk. I trudged the final steps to the top where I sat soaking up the fall sunshine until my heart calmed. I ate an apple and drank some water. How could I describe what had happened to me? What catchword would capture the essence of the experience? Faith. Trust. Love. Belief. Confidence. Hope. Positive thought. Intention. Focus. Never quitting. Never giving in. Never saying never. As I had searched for the breakthrough event, I would continue to search for the right words and never truly find them.

I explored a higher, steeper ridge east of the ranch with few trees and a southern exposure that kept its summit mostly snow free even during winter. This became my newest Mecca. The place had no name and I gave it none. From the ranch house, I strolled past the barn and corrals to traverse a dirt track along the river before branching off into a welter of knee-high sagebrush and downed-log drift fence. When I reached the five-wire fence that separated our property from the neighbor's, I loosened the second wire from the top of one post to create an easy entry and exit. Sacred places, those that provide an elevated view, know no boundaries and harbor no rules. If I trespassed, as surely I did, the hawks flying overhead pardoned me. Plus, I doubted that the landowners would ever come to that remote, difficult-to-access spot.

From the fence line, I followed old sheep and cattle trails to the base of the ridge, paused for one long-held breath and then began my ascent. In the beginning I had to stop every twenty-five breaths, then fifty, then a hundred. Before I left the ranch for good, I could climb to the top without stopping. I always arrived breathless and sweating. I always paused to settle my heart before I stepped into a small carved-out spot in the natural stone where I stood as if in front of an altar to pray to each of the four directions. Sometimes I stayed for minutes, sometimes for hours. Sometimes I hauled my sleeping bag up to stay the night and watch the moon in its relentless pursuit of perfection. There in the silence, far away from the haunts of other humans, I discovered that I was alone but not lonely, that I was apart but not separate from the world. I always descended the ridge with a renewed sense of purpose and the quiet satisfaction of knowing that all would be well no matter what happened. I had come to the same kind of sweet acceptance with my writing life: I would write the stories and poems that moved me. I would continue to believe that publication would come when the time was right, if ever.

I sought out other places to climb: alone to the top of Black Mountain, with a friend to the Limber Pine fantasy world outside of Fairplay. I returned to the Grand Canyon with a guide for a long weekend of sleeping by the river and climbing the cliffs. When my marriage ended and I was forced to leave the ranch, the last thing I did was scale the high ridge to pray for continued guidance and bury the collection of sacred objects I had gathered over fourteen years: antlers, arrowheads, flint chips, feathers, beads, and special stones. What the earth had given me, I returned with a grateful heart.

Another man embraced me. With his encouragement, other places called me: Lovell Gulch, Pine Springs, Guadalupe Peak, Hunter Peak, The Bowl, Bear Canyon, Dog Canyon, Mescalero Camp, Seminole Canyon, Fenton Lake, Enchanted Rock, Wichita Mountains, Chickasaw National Recreation Area, Woolly Hollow, Diamond Head in Hawaii, 3,000 miles through Mexico, a week's sailing adventure in the Virgin Islands. Even campgrounds, RV parks, roadside rest areas, and Walmart parking lots provided unobstructed and entertaining views of life. Every elevation, from sea level to the highest peak in Texas, offered me something to learn, someway to grow, some treasure to uncover, some delicacy to savor, some memory to cherish.

What is a landscape but a place to discover? What is a blank piece of paper except an opportunity to create? How will I know what is there until I go? How will I know the end of the poem or the story until I write the line or sentence that brings closure? If finding myself meant dedicating fifty-plus years of ongoing struggle to reach the summit so I could see forever, then finding the right words and working hard to perfect craft is nothing more than the ever-expanding process of going higher, of raising the "personal best" bar for literary and creative excellence.

While I dream of climbing Pikes Peak or some other Colorado fourteener, I don't mind the practice of strolling around the neighborhood, or setting my sights on more accessible ridges. While I still fervently pray for good health and healing, I acknowledge my limitations and listen to what my body needs. While I appreciate awards and recognition, what I really relish is the everyday exploratory training of writing simply to see what I might discover about myself, or the world at large. And while I'm happy if one of my books is published and finds an audience, I'm even more thrilled to help another writer find their authentic voice or develop a genuine style. I've said that all a writer needs is passion, patience and persistence. I would add perspective to that list.

Perspective is everything. Though you can only be where you are in any given moment, it helps to know where you've been and where you want to go. Rather like standing on a ridge top to look down at where you started, then gazing upward at the tallest peaks where you long to go. If climbing for the elevated view taught me anything, it taught me that roads and trails and paths are everywhere, and that I was never really lost, never truly trapped. All I had to do to release myself into the freedom of full expression was to keep seeking the light and believe, without doubt, in open doors.

## About the Editor

W.C. Jameson is the author of more than sixty-five books, 1,500 published articles and essays, dozens of poems, and three hundred songs. He has written and performed in a musical, acted in five films, and has appeared on the History Channel, the Discovery Channel, the Travel Channel, *Nightline*, PBS, and NPR. An award-winning songwriter, he has recorded five CDs, and written the soundtracks for one feature film and two documentaries. He currently travels the country performing at folk festivals, college campuses, roadhouses, and on television. When he is not on the road, he can be found in his writing studio in Llano, Texas.

CPSIA information can be obtained at www.ICGtesting.com
Printed in the USA
236368LV00002B/1/P